Connect-Five

Family learning and Every Child Matters

edited by Penny Lamb, Clare Meade, Rachel Spacey and Mandy Thomas

promoting adult learning

© 2007 National Institute of Adult Continuing Education
(England and Wales)
21 De Montfort Street
Leicester
LE1 7GE

Company registration no. 2603322
Charity registration no. 1002775

NIACE has a broad remit to promote lifelong learning opportunities for adults.
NIACE works to develop increased participation in education and training,
particularly for those who do not have easy access because of class, gender,
age, race, language and culture, learning difficulties or disabilities, or insufficient
financial resources.

ISBN 978 1 86201 326 1

You can find NIACE online at www.niace.org.uk

Cataloguing in Publication Data

A CIP record of this title is available from the British Library

Designed and typeset by Book Production Services

Printed in England by Latimer Trend, Plymouth

Contents

Acknowledgements

This publication would not have been possible without the help, support and encouragement of many people. We would like to give our thanks to family learning colleagues and learners across England who have shared their expertise, practice and experiences.

We would also like to thank colleagues from the Learning and Skills Council and Department of Innovation, Universities and Skills for their support with this publication.

The publication is funded by the Learning and Skills Council.

The editors gratefully acknowledge the help of the following individuals and institutions who supplied illustrations for this book:

Page 1: Leicestershire County Council; page 7: Isle of Wight Council Extended Services and Family Learning & Support Hub; page 17: Oldham Lifelong Learning Service; page 29: Peterborough College of Adult Education; page 30: Newcastle Document Service; page 34: Peterborough College of Adult Education: Peter Kirby and Alex Kirby-Lambert; page 40: Leicestershire County Council; page 47: Shutterstock; page 48: Leicestershire County Council; page 55: Malvern Hills Outdoor Education Centre; page 63: Malvern Hills Outdoor Education Centre; page 72: Leicestershire County Council; page 78: Leicestershire County Council; page 87: Leicestershire County Council; page 94: Cheshire County Council.

Foreword

We want to give everyone the best possible learning opportunities: to give them the best possible start in life, to ensure that they have the chance to pursue successful and rewarding careers and to help them live full and active lives as they approach retirement and beyond.

This is why the government is committed to learning for people of all ages and backgrounds and to creating a culture of learning in this country that bridges the generations. This theme is central to our policies and reforms, from *Every Child Matters*, the development of Children's Centres and Extended Schools and our wider reforms in schools, through the continuing development of post-16 education and training, improving access to Higher Education, and maintaining our commitment to Personal and Community Development Learning, to our determination to give this country the strong skills base envisaged by Lord Leitch.

I believe that Family Learning Programmes have a vital part to play in all this: in helping us to create a lifetime of opportunities for everyone, while building greater social cohesion and economic prosperity. Family learning supports inter-generational learning and helps create stronger family units and more joined up communities. By encouraging parents and carers to get involved in their children's learning, family learning helps adults to develop the skills and confidence to share in children's learning and to gain from that experience the confidence to learn for themselves.

The Family Literacy, Language and Numeracy (FLLN) initiative has been highly successful in delivering lasting improvements in literacy, language and numeracy skills for both children and their parents. We know that through these programmes, many adults gain the necessary skills to move back into employment. Over the coming year, we will be developing a number of new programmes including a programme that includes work experience to support parents returning to work. We will also be developing a FLLN course for parents of children aged 0-4 based on the Early Years Foundation Stage. We aim to extend the reach of FLLN by developing programmes to support foster carers, spouses of migrant workers, refugees and members of faith communities and will be building on the successful pilots which have engaged teenage parents and grandparents. We have also made a commitment to continue the regional FLLN adviser programme which is making an important contribution to improving the quality of FLLN provision.

It is critical that when we are funding learning programmes for some of the most vulnerable families in the country, that we know that they will receive a high quality learning experience the first time they walk through the door. This guide shows us many new and, innovative approaches developed by colleagues across the country that have done just that. I am certain that these will become building blocks of local practice. The challenge now is to build on what we have learned through this project to benefit all communities.

DAVID LAMMY MP

Minister for Skills in the Department for Innovation, Universities and Skills

Introduction and overview

Penny Lamb, NIACE

In a rapidly changing world of policy, practice and priorities it is often hard to keep ahead of current developments. This guide showcases examples of best practice from the field of family learning. Colleagues from across England share their ideas, enthusiasm and programmes. They demonstrate how family learning plays a vital role locally in meeting the new agendas for integrated education and social care provision as part of the *Every Child Matters* changes, as well as developing adult skills and building a culture of learning in families. Family learning's contribution to the five holistic themes – be healthy, stay safe, enjoy and achieve, make a positive contribution, and achieve economic well-being – are shared from a variety of perspectives. The wealth of material in this guide supports the promotion of the critical and vital role of family learning within the new agendas for children, young people and families. Family learning is certainly a field that punches above its weight in achievements!

The guide opens with a whistle-stop tour of the policy context. The multitude of policy documents (see references section) shows that this is not an area for the faint-hearted! However, the key message from family learning practitioners is that whatever the policy, whatever the changes, the experience of the learner, both adult and child, is at the centre of all they do. This works best where the provision is supported by a clear strategic direction and a recognition of the importance of this work to support the new agendas. Family learning sits at the critical interface of learning for adults as parents and carers, and learning for children. But it is more than just the two parts: the integration of learning for adults and children in the family setting leads to long-term changes in families, and the start of many new learning journeys.

Sue Evans' section on the planning of programmes highlights the critical element of making strategic links and placing programmes in the local context of the work of partner organisations. The section highlights the need to understand the data thoroughly and local needs analysis, to make sure that resources are being effectively used, to provide a curriculum in the places, and to the families where we can make the most difference. Colleagues in Solihull share methods of consulting with parents and carers as they developed their multi-agency family learning partnership. Oldham's Lifelong Learning service provides a thorough and imaginative approach to planning programmes for diversity. They share their expertise on developing distance learning packages to reach out to learners with diverse needs. The chapter is full of practical experiences and tips and provides a useful checklist to support colleagues to develop similar approaches.

The third and fourth sections of the guide provide two types of case studies: cross-cutting case studies and specific case studies linked to the *Every Child Matters* outcomes. Each section contains both in-depth studies exploring aspects of an issue, and shorter 'cameo' pieces to show good and developing practice. All contributors share the fundamentals of their approaches: a delight for others to dip into, imitate or adapt.

The white paper *Care Matters: time for change* (DfES, 2007a) sets out a radical package of priorities for change to improve the outcomes for looked-after children. The family learning service and partners in Newcastle share their work on ensuring engagement with foster carers and looked-after children in family learning provision. The case study explores the challenges of ensuring that provision is accessible, relevant and enables achievement for this unique group of families. Colleagues in Brighton share the details of their parenting skills programmes which embed literacy skills whilst working alongside health visitors and family support workers.

The critical role of the arts in family learning is explored. Peterborough College of Adult Education's family sculpture programme shows the fun of learning new skills together as a family, including collecting branches from the local woods to make a tarantula's legs! Camden Adult and Community Learning Service and partners use imaginative methods of using art and galleries to identify and celebrate family relationships. Birmingham Adult Education Service shares methods of developing a play script with 2–3 year-olds and parents to enhance communication, language and literacy skills, as well as providing access to the rich experience of theatre. Whilst in Richmond upon Thames the family learning service, working in partnership with the Orleans House Gallery, used a course of discussion and drawing-based sessions, 'Every Drawing Matters', to enable local families to become involved in the consultations of the borough's introduction of the new structures for *Every Child Matters*.

The importance of joint work between family learning and library services to encourage dads and male carers to stay in touch with their families whilst in custody is shown in case studies from Lincolnshire and Cumbria. In Lincoln Prison, inmates chose books from a Read Together collection in the prison library and a duplicate copy is sent to the families' local library. The Libraries and Learning Service makes contact with the family and supports them to access the book dad has chosen and support the families with literacy support. Dads and children exchange letters about the books and share story-telling activities on prison visits. At Haverigg Prison in Cumbria the Family Learning Service and the Library service develop the skills of dads and male carers in story telling and developing strategies for working with children to enhance learning and development. The men produce a CD-ROM with stories and messages for their children.

Colleagues in Oxfordshire and Somerset provide imaginative responses to family learning programmes for cultural minority families. The Family Learning Service at Oxfordshire County Council has developed a customised programme of Keeping Up with the Children that bridges links between home and school cultures. The learners wanted to be more involved in the school and community, and wanted to share their experiences of being Pakistani Muslim women living in Oxford. They decided to write a booklet together reflecting their lives and experiences and to present the booklet to the school for sharing with staff, children and other families. The programme became a two-way exchange between the school and families. Somerset County Council Family Learning Service provide a structured course covering reading, writing, speaking and listening that encourages families to work together and work towards integration and understanding of school life.

Many programmes address the importance of the relationship between family learning and all five of the *Every Child Matters* outcomes:

Be healthy gives the opportunity for a positive approach to supporting families in their physical, emotional and social well-being. Family learning programmes not only develop an understanding of improving health within families, but also between communities, for example exploring healthy cuisines across cultures. The 'Being Healthy' programme in Stockton has been formed from converging local needs. It was developed using a whole-person approach to health and learning, including community-based healthy eating sessions, and programmes that support parents in gaining skills to support their child's healthy development through social and emotional education. York Family Learning Service, in partnership with SureStart, supports parents and carers to prepare and share a meal with their children, as well as improving literacy skills and producing a cookbook. The Sunderland Family Adult and Community Learning team show an exciting method of reaching families who would not normally access learning opportunities through Family Football coaching programmes.

Stay safe is at the heart of the *Every Child Matters* agenda. There is a focus on all agencies ensuring the child and his / her experience is the centre of how services are provided. The input of parents and carers at every stage is critical. Family learning programmes have supported families to challenge positively issues around bullying, substance abuse and antisocial behaviour. Other programmes have focused on personal safety. The Family Learning Service on the Isle of Wight provide an excellent example of how parents have shaped and supported the design of a programme on how the youth justice system works and what it means to families, with the aim of keeping children and young people safe from crime and anti-social behaviour. As the team say: 'something that you think might work is an innovation, and a calculated risk is a pilot!' Lancashire Adult Learning service team with the Road Safety Group run a Stay Safe programme for parents and carers. The Swindon Learning Partnership have developed a Family Health and Safety programme provided through 'Supporting Our Kids' clubs in schools, children's centres and family centres.

Family learning has a unique and essential contribution to make towards **Enjoy and achieve** in ensuring parents and carers feel confident to play their part as the fundamental influence and first educators of their children. Families learning together establish a culture of learning and achievement that lasts a lifetime. Knowsley Family and Community Education (FACE) provide an inspirational example of their targeted work with the 'Juskidz' programme. This is a partnership project providing family learning with a self-help group that offers respite and support to parents and carers of children with physical disabilities and/or learning difficulties. The project illustrates an example of an effective curriculum developed and evolved around the needs of the families and at the right pace for the group. St Helens Adult and Community Learning Service share their model of ensuring learning through play. Bournemouth Adult Learning use 'Fun with Words' to provide an enjoyable family literacy programme, whilst Worcestershire County Council family learning team describe how local families take to the Malvern Hills for outdoor activity family learning weekends, including orienteering, photo trails and storytelling.

As part of **Making a positive contribution,** family learning can play a critical role in supporting and encouraging positive social behaviour. Wakefield's Family SEAL project shows how parents can support the development of children's social, emotional and behavioural skills and gain adult literacy skills at the same time. West Sussex County Council provide an example of how they encourage parents to become involved in learning by providing support in their children's school whilst also taking an accredited programme. Hampshire County Council Adult and Community Learning Service facilitate a programme entitled 'Learning Together about Children's Rights'. It raises awareness amongst families about the United Nations Convention on the Rights of the Child. Much lively debate ensues about the impact and implications on family life!

Our final case studies illustrate the theme of **Achieve economic well-being.** Socio-economic disadvantages in families and communities create major obstacles to all facets of well-being. Family learning is often the first step in giving parents and carers new skills to move into training and employment. The example from Leicestershire County Council illustrates just this, the powerful starting point of a learning journey: Sally, a local parent moves through a family learning programme, on to further learning and into a career as a plumber and away from a life on benefits. This case study shows the ethos of the school is critical in enabling the first step onto the learning ladder. Lancashire Adult Learning Service share how parents take the first steps from a Keeping Up with the Children programme, on to family literacy, numeracy and language programmes and then on to the local college. Redbridge Institute of Adult Education give an effective example of working with the local Refugee Forum to provide both family learning and sewing classes for local Somali families. Kingston Adult Education Family Learning Service illustrate how they have built a 'Springboard' course as a progression route from family learning programmes to support further learning and career opportunities.

Finally the guide looks at the quality improvement agenda across family learning and the *Every Child Matters* outcomes. The examples in this guide show how colleagues are working with some of the most vulnerable families, often with a deep-seated fear of schools and bad experiences of learning. We sometimes only have one chance to re-engage a family in learning: if we do not provide a high-quality learning experience the first time that the family plucks up courage to walk through the door, then we may lose them forever. Cheshire County Council share their model of a quality framework and how this is used in the North West.

So whether you come to this guide as a provider, a manager, a policy maker or a curious reader, we can guarantee that the examples included of practice from across the country will lift your spirits and provide inspiration. They will also show that programmes do not always have to be new or innovative to be effective, the basics of many of the examples can be simply replicated. The essence is the power of the family as a learning unit to make long-term and sustainable changes.

Section 1
THE POLICY CONTEXT

Be Healthy
Parents, carers & families
promote healthy choices.

Get out into the fresh air.
Take up a new sport.

St Mary's Health
Promotion Unit
Tel: 814284
Leisure Activities
Tel: 821000

Enjoy and Achieve
Parents, carers & families
support learning.
Have you thought about
you today? Want to learn
something new?
Adult & Community Learning
Service Tel: 823822
Isle of Wight College
Tel: 526631

Make a Positive Contribution
Parents, carers & families promote
positive behaviour.

What skills can you offer? Be a school Governor.
Join your school Friends Association.
Be a volunteer.

Rural Community Council Tel: 524058
Island School Governors Tel: 823458

Stay Safe
Parents, carers & families
provide safe homes & stability.

Do you know where your children are?
Do you know who they are with?

NSPCC
Helpline Tel:
0808 800 5000
FIZ Tel:
821999

Achieve Economic Well Being
Parents, carers & families are
supported to be economically active.

Looking ahead? Looking for training?
Looking for work?

Job Centre Plus Tel: 276627
Next Step Tel: 0791 921 5249

These are a series of fridge magnets produced by Isle of Wight Council Extended Services and Family Learning and Support Hub.

Every Child Matters and family learning: the policy context

Penny Lamb and Rachel Spacey, NIACE

In this chapter we give an overview of the policy developments that have helped to shape and develop family learning over the past decade. The family is seen increasingly as a fundamental conduit for social policy, as the means through which both current and future generations influence and shape the society around them. Learning through the family is, therefore, being gradually recognised as a positive way of engaging families consciously in this process and helping them to take control of their lives and futures.

Family learning: how it developed

Family learning's short but rich history draws on a number of traditions, including adult literacy, early learning, lifelong learning, parenting, parental involvement, school improvement and supporting children's learning. From the 1970s to the 1990s family literacy, language and numeracy programmes were developed mainly within the context of adult literacy. During the 1990s research demonstrated the intergenerational effects of poor literacy and numeracy, resulting in the decision to fund national demonstration programmes, grants to local programmes and in-depth longitudinal and case study research. *A Fresh Start – improving literacy and numeracy* (DfEE, 1999b) highlighted the effectiveness of family literacy, language and numeracy programmes in engaging parents and tackling poor skills in families. Equally, a tradition of a wider curriculum with children and parents learning together was developed through sports, arts, regeneration and community initiatives.

From the late 1990s, local authorities were supported to develop family literacy and family numeracy programmes through the DfES standards funds. The responsibility for planning and funding of programmes transferred to the Learning and Skills Council in 2002.

There are two distinct types of programmes that make up the LSC's family programmes: family literacy, language (which includes families for whom english is an additional language) and numeracy programmes; and wider family learning programmes. The latter aim to encourage local authorities to engage families in learning together over a range of curriculum areas.

Every Child Matters: safeguarding every child

At the heart of current government policies around families and children are the themes of social justice and opportunity for all. Family programmes are seen as a key factor in moving this forward, and as a building block of social mobility. Family learning plays its part in contributing to a number of different policy areas. Earlier work by NIACE[1] illustrates how the programmes link across and contribute to Public Service Agreement targets for children and families, Skills for Life, Museums, Libraries and Archives, health improvement, skills and economic competitiveness to name just a few.

Every Child Matters (HM Government, 2003) and *Every Child Matters: change for children* (HM Government, 2004b) set out the government's agenda for change to improve outcomes for all children and young people, and to provide a national framework for all local authorities to lead the change programmes.

The key element of the policy is to bring together all services for children in a locality across health, welfare and education, to ensure that no child falls through the net between services. It is a radical outcomes-based framework and, whilst local authorities are given the lead role to enable the change agenda to take place, they are tasked to engage with other statutory, voluntary and community services and to create Children's Trusts to formalise joint working arrangements by 2008. The list of key players is extensive and includes public, voluntary, private and independent sectors, housing, early years services, children's centres, schools, play services, transport, leisure services, Primary Care Trusts, GPs and health services, education and social services.

A range of further policy documents and guidance illustrate how the new agenda will be implemented in health settings (DfES and DoH, 2004), in schools (DfES, 2004a), in social care (DfES, 2004b), in the criminal justice system (Home Office, 2004), in youth services (HM Government, 2005b) and for Children in Care (DfES, 2006a; DfES, 2007a). Along with this comes guidance on ensuring that systems link together and that there is a reduction in unnecessary bureaucracy. (DfES and Cabinet Office, 2005).

---

[1] Haggart and Spacey (2006a).

All services are tasked to work together to achieve a new vision for children and families based on five fundamental outcomes for children:

- Be healthy,
- Stay safe,
- Enjoy and achieve,
- Make a positive contribution,
- Achieve economic well-being.

Extending the role of schools

Within the same Change for Children package, schools are required to further develop a range of extended services to build stronger relationships with parents and the wider community. This builds on earlier policy initiatives removing the barriers from schools in providing support for communities and families (HM Government, 2002) and the extended schools pathfinder projects in 25 local authorities in 2002–03.[2] The DfES five-year strategy (DfES, 2004d) made a universal commitment for primary age children and their families to a closer relationship between parents and schools. The extended schools prospectus (DfES, 2005b) set out the core offer of extended services that it is hoped all children will be able to access through schools by 2010. The core offer for mainstream and special schools is outlined below. Family learning sessions are included as part of the core offer.

The core offer for mainstream and special schools

- High quality 'wraparound' childcare provided on the school site or through other local providers, with supervised transfer arrangements where appropriate, available 8 a.m.–6 p.m. all year round.

- A varied menu of activities to be on offer, such as homework clubs and study support, sport (at least two hours a week beyond the school day for those who want it), music tuition, dance and drama, arts and crafts, special interest clubs such as chess and first aid courses, visits to museums and galleries, learning a foreign language, volunteering, business and enterprise activities.

2. Haggart and Spacey (2006c).

- Parenting support, including information sessions for parents at key transition points, parenting programmes run with the support of other children's services and family learning sessions to allow children to learn with their parents.

- Swift and easy referral to a wide range of specialist support services such as speech therapy, child and adolescent mental health services, family support services, intensive behaviour support, and (for young people) sexual health services. Some may be delivered on school sites.

- Providing wider community access to ICT, sports and arts facilities, including adult learning.

Extended Schools: Access to opportunities and services for all (DfES 2005b)

The recent publication, *Extended Schools: building on experience* (DCSF, 2007) outlines the initial impact of the policy in the first 5,000 schools offering full-range extended services. It records improvements in attainment and in motivation and engagement in learning for some pupils from disadvantaged backgrounds and shares examples of best practice. There is a further commitment to increase funding for enhancing the coordination and sustainability of extended services over the next three years.

The role of Children's Centres

Similarly, SureStart Children's Centres are at the heart of the *Every Child Matters* programme. Health services and Jobcentre Plus in particular have a strong role to play in working with local authorities to improve health and well-being and reduce disadvantage. They provide integrated multi-agency services and are a universal point of access for early learning and childcare, family support, health services, support into employment, and links to other specialist services. SureStart Children's Centres aim to improve outcomes for all children, but place a particular focus on the most disadvantaged. The government is committed to providing 3,500 SureStart Children's Centres, one in every community, by 2010.

The core offer for SureStart Children's Centres to be in place by 2010

To offer or provide access to:

• In centres in the 30 per cent most disadvantaged areas: integrated early learning and childcare (early years provision) for a minimum of 10 hours a day, five days a week, 48 weeks a year; and support for a childminder network. Or:

• In centres in the 70 per cent least disadvantaged areas, which do not elect to offer early years provision: drop-in activity sessions for children, such as stay and play sessions.

• Family Support, including support and advice on parenting, information about services available in the area and access to specialist, targeted services; and Parental Outreach.

• Child and Family Health Services, such as antenatal and postnatal support, information and guidance on breastfeeding, health and nutrition, smoking cessation support, and speech and language therapy and other specialist support.

• Links with Jobcentre Plus to encourage and support parents and carers who wish to consider training and employment.

• Quick and easy access to wider services.

Governance Guidance for SureStart Children's Centres and Extended Schools (DfES, 2007c)

The revised practice guidance for SureStart Children's Centres (DfES and DoH, 2006) includes family learning programmes under its description of employment support, whilst it is included as part of parenting support in the Extended Schools Core offer.

Workforce reform

Workforce reform is a key plank of the new agendas. Bentley and O'Leary (2006) argue:

If outcomes for children are to improve then the change must take root in the everyday interactions between professionals, young people, families and communities. This requires considerable changes in professionals' practice ... requiring professionals to understand their roles through the prism of outcomes for children rather than by particular professional practice or practitioner groupings. (p. 21)

Every Child Matters reforms have introduced a common assessment framework and the requirement to share information amongst professionals. The Common Core of Skills and Knowledge for the Children's Workforce sets out the knowledge needed by people (including volunteers) whose work brings them into regular contact with children, young people and families.

The Children's Workforce Development Council supports the implementation of local integrated children's workforce strategies. A range of National Occupational Standards for care, for the children's workforce, and for working with parents and family learning now exist. Units of accreditation are being developed from these standards.

The *Respect Action Plan* (Home Office, 2006) announced the establishment of the National Academy for Parenting Practitioners (NAPP), due to be launched in October 2007. NAPP's role is to support the training and development for the Parenting workforce, act as a national centre for advice and research on parenting and parenting support and to support the government's developing parenting agenda.

Equally, there is reform to the qualifications frameworks for those working to develop the skills of parents and carers as adult learners. From September 2007, all new teachers in the publicly funded lifelong learning sector will be expected to have completed the Preparing to Teach in the Lifelong Learning Sector (PTLLS) course. They will then be expected to work towards a further teaching award appropriate to their role. The requirement for literacy, numeracy and ESOL teachers to qualify as specialists will continue.

Linking with the Change for Children agenda is the Step Into Learning programme. This is aimed at equipping staff in nurseries and SureStart Children's Centres with the knowledge and skills to help them identify parents' and carers' literacy, language and numeracy needs and support them into local provision. Training was delivered to staff based on a cascade model. The programme also supported staff with their own needs. It was centrally funded by the Skills for Life Strategy Unit and the SureStart Unit until March 2006. There is now an expectation that it is funded locally, with the original staff target group being widened, so that at least parts of the programme are delivered to different agencies, including extended schools partnerships.

Skills for Families

Running in a parallel development between 2003 and 2005 was the national Skills for Families initiative. This was a joint initiative between the Learning and Skills Council and the Skills for Life Strategy Unit and managed by the Basic Skills Agency. It aimed to develop strategic approaches to extending and embedding quality family, literacy, language and numeracy programmes through building an infrastructure, testing new approaches to programmes and training, disseminating good practice and producing useful resources for practitioners. In the first year (2003–04) 12 local authority / LSC partnerships received additional funding to build capacity, and in the second year a further seven partnerships joined the initiative. This initiative has been followed in 2006 by a programme of regional family literacy, numeracy and language advisers now managed by the Quality Improvement Agency. The advisers are also expert practitioners in local authorities.

The skills agenda

Family literacy, language and numeracy programmes support the development of skills for parents and carers and the programmes have made significant achievements towards the national Skills for Life targets. The Leitch review of skills (December 2006) focuses on the need for skills for economic prosperity and whilst it recognises the links between educational attainment and family background, there is as yet scant policy direction on engaging adults and families into learning to build social cohesion and social mobility.

Focus on families

The Respect agenda runs in a parallel policy development to *Every Child Matters*. Along with the introduction of NAPP, The *Respect Action Plan* (Home Office, 2006) has a focus on antisocial behaviour. It provides a clear steer on supporting families, improving behaviour and attendance in schools, developing a new approach to what it defines as the 'most challenging families'. From that plan, a national network of family intervention projects has been established using long-term, multi-agency strategies for families needing high levels of support.

The Social Exclusion Task Force review for families at risk has published its first report, *Reaching Out: Think Family* (Cabinet Office Social Exclusion Team, 2007). The report reinforces the positive effects of intergenerational learning and the significant impact that the level of parental interest in a child's education has in raising attainment. It identifies the need to 'Think Family' both in terms of providing a tailored flexible service to the individual family with multiple needs and in terms of service structures. It identifies the significant opportunities to extend the *Every Child Matters* approach of integrated provision beyond children's services to all services, including adult services and working with families at risk.

A key theme running through the change agenda is a renewed policy interest in the importance of the role of parents in supporting their children's learning, in relation to improving their children's behaviour and in shaping the new services in localities. Guidance to Local Authorities has been issued on Parenting Support, on the nomination of a Parenting Commissioner and financial support provided to develop a Local Authority Parenting Strategy.

Every Parent Matters (DfES, 2007b) sets out the policy initiatives promoting the development of services for parents and the actions needed to involve parents in the shaping of services for families. In addition, it outlines forthcoming initiatives in this area. A £40 million national pilot for Parenting Support Advisers (PSAs) is being introduced in over 600 schools across 20 local authorities with the highest indices of deprivation. A wider roll-out is planned in 2008. New pilots have been introduced in selected local authorities to support parents of young children to develop and support at-home learning.

Continuing change

Announcements made in July 2007 widen the types of family literacy, language and numeracy programmes: for early years settings, for foster carers and their children, family language programmes to meet the needs of spouses of migrant workers, refugees and members of faith communities, for parents wanting to move back into employment.

Prior to finalising this guide, the new Prime Minister, Gordon Brown, has restructured the Department for Education and Skills into two new departments: The Department for Children, Schools and Families (DCSF) and the Department for Innovation, Universities and Skills (DIUS). The Respect agenda moves from the Home Office to the DCSF.

The case studies on the following pages illustrate how family learning practitioners have embraced the new policy agendas and, building on their long-established background of multi-agency working, are operating across the boundaries of learning for adults and learning for children.

Section 2
PLANNING THE PROGRAMMES

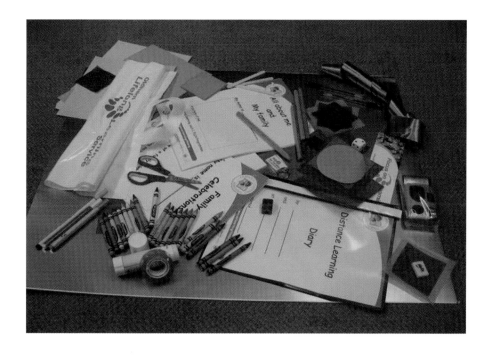

Needs analysis, consulting with learners and using data

Sue Evans, Family Learning Consultant

The beauty and burden of *Every Child Matters* (ECM)[3] is that no one organisation can possibly deliver it all on its own. It is a strategy that reaches every aspect of our communities and, if family learning is to play a full part, we need to understand what work is already going on and how we can add to its impact. If you have any doubts about the role your organisation and programmes can play in these changes, look at www.everychildmatters.gov.uk, with its stress on inter-agency working, alongside NIACE's *Linking the Thinking* (Haggart and Spacey, 2006a). Furthermore, the Department of Communities and Local Government (DCLG) www.communities.gov.uk has a raft of targets and objectives, many linked to ECM, centred on regeneration and community development. Clearly, family learning has much to offer – our challenge is to develop the programmes and attract the learners who will benefit most from these reforms.

Putting your work in a context

The first step in any needs analysis is to look at what information has already been gathered. As we are looking to contribute to a much wider agenda there is more information available and we must look beyond traditional learning providers to other key stakeholders. Does the local authority have a local area agreement (LAA)? What about children and young people's services, or the health trust? Is there demographic trend information or statistics from the government regional office? Try the LSC regional commissioning plan for the area and speak to any voluntary sector organisations or networks that may have carried out local research. The information should give an outline of the needs and challenges in your area – next you need to colour it in…

Talking to your learners

The key to a good needs analysis is not to assume that your constituents want more of what they already have. Give your partners and learners room to make

3 HM Government (2004b)

proactive suggestions and use a range of approaches to reach the widest audience. Some people may be happy to respond to a web or paper-based consultation but others will need the help of a learning champion or outreach worker. Be bold in what you ask. Explore possible combinations of programmes and information sessions, talk about personal and community aspirations, confidence and even qualifications! In the Solihull Family Learning Network example (Cameo 1, p. 22), Trish Botten describes how they use a programme of seminars and conferences to consult directly with learners and other providers. Like this, the best learner consultation is an ongoing process and an integral part of the planning, monitoring and evaluation of programmes. Evaluation may be the end of one programme, but it is the start of a new cycle of needs analysis and curriculum development.

Understanding what's already in place

Numerous organisations will be running awareness and education programmes in any given area at any given time, so try to map out the provision that is already available. Bear in mind that some areas may be suffering from 'initiative overload' because socio-economic indicators mean they attract the most public funding. If this is the case you either need to be especially creative in complementing the existing provision, or take the decision to work with a priority group that is getting less direct attention. 'Deprivation based' funding can mean that areas with high variations, or tiny pockets of need, are overlooked and such gaps need to be identified and addressed.

Collecting and using data

Data analysis is only useful if you have collected the right data in the first place. If your management information systems are weak, then you will be missing a fundamental tool in the evaluation of existing programmes and the planning of new ones. It is easy to think of learner data as nothing more than an accounting tool and a chore. If you collect the bare minimum to satisfy external requirements, that may be true, but if you consider carefully what you ask your learners and how you record their answers, you could arm yourself with a powerful management tool.

Alongside needs analysis, your data can tell you everything, from whether your courses are delivered at the right time to whether your marketing strategy is working. Postcode analysis can help to identify gaps in recruitment. Success rates may show you whether your programme has been key in achieving, or making progress towards, an ECM outcome. Be aware of the range of services and support that your learners access and try to understand the significance (big or small) of family learning in their achievements. They may have gained a certificate, but is life at home calmer? Are they now thinking of giving up smoking or getting a library card? You need to know, and so do your partners.

Curriculum planning – making the strategic links

Does ECM have anything to offer us in terms of the way we plan and develop our family learning programmes? It is hard to think of any existing family learning programme that will not fit into one of the five ECM themes (there's always 'Enjoy and achieve' if the others don't work!), but is there any strategic or practical value in showing how the two fit together?

This book shows how ECM can provide a clear context and recognisable language for negotiation with partners from museum staff to health visitors. Where *Linking the Thinking* (Haggart and Spacey, 2006a) demonstrated that family learning can contribute to a range of government targets, ECM gives a strategic framework to the curriculum we offer and the way in which we address the range of needs of the families in our communities, urging us to work with partners who have the same long term goals.

What am I trying to achieve? Who am I trying to reach?

Curriculum planning is about attaining a delicate equilibrium between the needs and wants of the families you intend to reach and the priorities that are set for you (e.g. by government, your management, your funding bodies). In an ideal world the two sides are the same but in reality the balance may be harder to achieve. Be clear about what you MUST deliver (minimum numbers etc.) and then think about your mission and objectives. You might feel that these are more valuable to your learners but you need to do both.

A successful programme is one that delivers what it set out to do, in terms of both immediate and longer term objectives. Every programme will have an immediate curriculum related objective – to become better at maths or art for example, but there will also be wider objectives and in inter-agency working, it is especially helpful to articulate these. Sometimes the participation of a particularly disenfranchised group in any type of learning seems like a significant achievement, but there is still value in looking across the ECM outcomes.

If you are working with the fire service to reduce household fires and with the health service to reduce smoking and improve infant mortality rates, you could decide to deliver a 'Staying safe–being healthy' programme to your target learners. At the end you will know about progression and achievement over the life of the programme, but later you may be able to describe other successes. A year on you may not know whether it was the cutting down in smoking (thanks to the health workers), free smoke alarms (from the fire service) or increased safety awareness (in your family learning programme) that reduced the number of children killed in domestic fires in your target area, but you should know if there has been a reduction – and if there has, that is a triumph, for all of you.

What programmes should I deliver? Is there a demand and a NEED for what I have done before? What new programmes should I develop?

Taking into account the views of learners and of your partners, you could identify key ECM themes. Consider whether your current curriculum is attracting the learners you were targeting and whether you need to change it. Are you looking at being healthy when the parents you want to reach are worried about staying safe? Is it time to link the two themes or involve a partner?

Who with?

Is there another key player in the area with similar or complementary objectives to yours? Your needs analysis and consultation will have highlighted organisations or networks that will help you reach out to your target learners. Could you help to arrange an ECM planning day and invite them along? The partners you choose will help you to contextualise your programmes. They may have access to specialist expertise or resources, they may have more or different funding (for equipment for example), they may just have more time. This level of strategic collaboration is at the heart of ECM.

When?

Use a planning calendar, thinking about the shape of the year. School terms obviously need to be noted but so do religious/cultural festivals, factory shutdowns, national or local campaign weeks. It's not just about avoiding certain times but actively joining in. Make the most of big local or national events, especially those that will attract media coverage – stop-smoking drives, sporting events, healthy-eating promotions, anti-bullying campaigns, cultural or historic festivals or even a local election. By designing and timing your programmes to coincide with these you may benefit from free venues and marketing while raising the profile of your service.

More information?

Curriculum development and planning is one of *The Building Blocks of Quality in Family Learning* (Haggart and Spacey, 2006b). See the reference section for details.

Cameo 1: Solihull Family Learning Network

Since the launch of the Solihull Family Learning Network in March 2005, the needs and views of our learners have become core to the way we plan and deliver family learning in Solihull. Learners have helped us to develop a vision for the network, a 'Strategy for Family Learning' in Solihull and an action plan to deliver our strategic objectives. They have told us what, for them, are the key factors for a positive learning experience, how the service could be improved and what else families would like to learn. Their views have influenced our curriculum planning and encouraged us to use more local venues.

We have consulted with a wide range of organisations and individuals through a programme of conferences and seminars, supported by information on our webpages. We also use Learning Champions in the Fordbridge area of Solihull, who have been out and about in the community, talking to local people, finding out what they would like to learn and where, and encouraging them to participate.

Underpinning the process of engagement with partners has been an innovative piece of commissioned consultation with families done for the Network by the Campaign for Learning (www.campaign-for-learning.org.uk). Ongoing family learning activities such as ceramics, drama and robotics were used to introduce fun visual prompts and group discussion. A puppet-making event at Chelmsley Wood Town Centre allowed us to consult with non-learners through the use of a 2 metre high thermometer – hot for positive comments and cold for barriers and things they thought could be improved.

Trish Botten, Solihull Family Learning Network

Planning For diversity: thinking good practice from the start

Mary R. Grainger, Oldham Lifelong Learning Service

What does diversity mean to us?

Diversity is an umbrella term, which recognises that everyone is different. It promotes respect for and recognition of this difference. In Oldham we are very clear that we need to look at both promoting and planning for diversity.

> Promoting diversity in your classroom should involve celebrating (as appropriate to the age group) those aspects of our lives that make us unique, for example: gender, ethnicity, religion, language, physical ability, age, lifestyle, family circumstances (social class), sexuality. (Lander, 2006).

It also involves planning to meet individual needs and checking progress.

Planning for diversity requires these differences to be taken into account and the curriculum to be planned around them. This is not necessarily the same as promoting diversity in the classroom. Our planning of the curriculum includes using local data on the achievement rates of schools and the need in Children's Centres together with the literacy, language and numeracy levels of adults. This may result in provision being offered in particular geographical areas or specific types of locations.

There are however, some 'communities' of learners who have particular needs, so, in order to reach those learners and their families, we have to think in different ways when planning to meet these diverse needs. For example, those of offenders, travellers, refugees and asylum seekers, young parents, men, shift workers, those in women's refuge or parents of or with special needs, looked-after children and grandparents. The example used in this section illustrates how, in Oldham, we have adapted the curriculum to meet the needs of a specific group of families from the black and minority ethnic (BME) community using distance-learning materials to support a flexible delivery model.

Thinking good practice from the start

Since 2001, fully aware of the impact that the acquisition of language has on community and social cohesion and on children's attainment, we have been keen to develop family learning with English for Speakers of Other Languages (ESOL) learners. In 2004 we noticed that there was a sharp drop-off of learners during Ramadan and Eid in a family learning class in Greenhill Primary School. An Ofsted report in 2006 noted that 'All the pupils live in the immediate area, which displays some features of disadvantage. All the pupils are from minority ethnic groups; 58 per cent come from Pakistani and 42 per cent from Bangladeshi backgrounds. Last year 74 per cent of the pupils entered school with no English language.' With the impetus from our involvement in Skills for Families and some additional funding we set out to see how we could meet the needs of this group.

Learner needs had been assessed generally during the previous courses held in the schools. The overall language levels had been at Entry Level 1 and Entry Level 2. The course was mapped to the ESOL curriculum, so we were aware of the language needs and the importance of the family in acquiring language and skills to support the children's learning.

Through discussions with tutors and learners, we had established that it was difficult to attend classes during Ramadan due to the additional commitments at home, such as cooking, prayer times, disrupted sleep patterns and fasting. Learners still wanted to attend classes but felt that they needed more flexibility and less pressure of fixed classroom times.

Working with the school staff, the bilingual support workers and the learners we developed a distance-learning pack to try to meet these needs. The first pilot course was developed and delivered by Janet McDowell, Programme Leader for Family Learning, who has an ESOL background. This has since been 'rolled-out' to other schools over the last three years and to date 95 families have been engaged in learning during Ramadan and Eid through distance-learning courses.

How it works: the overview

The learners attend five flexible sessions and take home a pack of distance-learning materials. The 'topics' of the sessions are negotiated with the learners based on their interests and the things that they would like to do to support their own learning of the language and to help their children. The areas they wished to develop in order to become more involved in the community and in school life were School, Home, and Me and My Family. In addition, the topic of festivals and celebrations, covering a range of cultural festivals, was added.

Learners complete the activities and record them in a diary in text and by using a disposable camera. Flexible attendance to suit learners during Ramadan and Eid is negotiated and a language-support team engaged to support learners by telephone during this period.

Teaching and learning

In the classroom

The adults learn how to use the camera, organise portfolios, take part in discussions, ask questions, show their own and their families' work to other learners and review learning in diaries and in course reflections, verbally and written. They learn how to complete activities before taking them home. Essentially, they identify what learning has taken place in the home within the family and their own role in that learning.

At home

Adults learn with their children and with other family members including their spouses and extended family members. The activity packs and resources facilitate learning together.

Adults became 'teachers' and 'learners'; they may have taught the young children how to complete a puzzle whilst older siblings taught them how to read a passage and answer questions correctly. They became facilitators in that they might provide an activity for a grandparent and his grandchildren to do together whilst the parent works with other children. The combination in extended families is endless!

The outcomes from this approach are stunning: it generates excitement, family involvement, improvement in speaking skills, and quality time spent together as a family, to name but a few.

Achievements and progression

Some of the learners could be defined as 'functionally illiterate', some had never attended school or had left at a very young age and most had never experienced the use of interactive and creative teaching materials and resources. By introducing them to the creativity of this distance-learning course, they were able to immerse themselves in the packs and enjoy and experience learning with their children and grandchildren. Some then went on to go out and buy more materials, again for the first time.

Learners' borrowing of books extended to using the local library and, as some learners had prams with them, they organised their own methods of taking home and storing resources safely.

Most of the learners progressed to the Share course in 2006, which continued with the home activity scheme but also developed understanding of the skills children are acquiring, for example, when counting or using scissors.

The adults progressed to a variety of courses, including classes in literacy and language, numeracy, ESOL, managing behaviour, family literacy, Share, IT, family keep fit and dance, 'Say it, Read it, Write it', and family learning workshops and festivals. Some of these courses lead to national qualifications. All courses are mapped to the National Standards for adult literacy, numeracy and ICT (QCA, 2005).

This is what we learnt

- It's possible to have **100 per cent retention and achievement and 90 per cent attendance during Ramadan.**
- That this model could be rolled-out, including to ESOL courses.
- It is **more expensive** to resource than other courses.
- This flexible way of working does engage learners and they are motivated to attend. It is much more than giving learners 'homework': **it is a new way of working with families.**
- An interesting pattern arose in that some learners were from the same extended families, therefore, **children were being 'shared'.** We became aware that one child may be asked to do the same activities by his grandma, his mother and his auntie. The bilingual support assistant had close knowledge of the families and was able to discuss the possibility of children becoming pressurised and overworked – or to check were they just pleased to be getting so much attention!

- **If a course is flexible** and takes into account special circumstances of a particular group such as religious celebrations and prayer times it will be successful.
- **Extended family members** attended the group sessions if the usual learner was unable to attend, i.e. fathers and grandparents. Even teenage brothers were joining in!
- We learned that classes do not have to focus on female carers and tutors only, and that male family members can embrace and enjoy the course as much as women! This established a pathway to developing courses for male carers into a variety of family learning courses and as partners in the Children's Centre.
- One **new male-only course** has attracted 12 male parents.
- Learners were enthusiastic and confident to **speak in English** about the activities they had completed with their family during the week and what they had learned together.
- They expressed a feeling of **achievement** supported by the photographs and diaries.
- **Families were working together** during Ramadan and Eid when parents tend to be extremely busy and tired.
- As with all initiatives **not everything goes to plan.**

Further information on Planning for Diversity and Oldham's flexible learning approach can be found at **www.niace.org.uk/connect-five**

A checklist from Oldham

Establishing the need: clearly identify the target group

- Use data etc. to identify those 'hard-to-reach' groups who are not being included in the 'main' programme.
- Identify how this fits in with strategic planning and *Every Child Matters* (ECM).
- Recognise the links to other initiatives, e.g. ECM, Community cohesion.

Knowledge of target group

- Undertake research from literature and practice.
- Have a clear understanding of the lifestyles, culture, religion and restrictions in terms of access etc. for the group.
- Identify specific barriers to learning for these families.

Choice of the relevant partners

- Identify key workers who have knowledge of the target group.
- Acknowledge the expertise of link workers.
- Plan partnership working and allow time for it.

Consultation/ finding out about the 'communities'

- Consult, involve a small group of 'target' learners and partners to inform planning.

Programme planning

- Decide the 'make-up' of the groups, e.g. single-sex.
- Agree length of courses and course dates.
- Ensure the accessibility of accommodation.
- Ensure SfL / FLLN specialist teachers available and trained.
- Organise to fit in with religious festivals etc.
- Plan with pre-16 teachers and post-16 teachers.
- Offer taster sessions.
- Agree promotion and marketing.

Curriculum negotiation and planning

- Identify interests of the group for topics/context.
- Negotiate relevant curriculum.
- Map courses to the curriculum and ECM outcomes.
- Decide involvement of children.
- Prepare home tasks for extended family members.
- Value home knowledge.
- Progression planning to mainstream.
- Opportunity for accreditation (including citizenship).
- Include promotion of diversity.

Additional support needed?

- Plan the use of bilingual support workers.
- Check if additional crèche facilities needed.
- Support from other workers, e.g. outreach, liaison workers etc.

Additional tasks

- Carry out health and safety risk assessments.
- Decide staff ratio.
- Ensure CRB checks carried out.
- Agree and plan trips/educational visits.

Assessing the success of the programme

- Ensure assessment criteria in place.
- Plan for accreditation.
- Progression mapped and 'follow up' strategies in place.
- Evaluations from learners and all partners.
- Plan celebrations.

Section 3
CROSS-CUTTING CASE STUDIES

This section shares case studies and smaller 'cameos', illustrating how family learning cuts across the five *Every Child Matters* themes.

Parenting skills and family learning: joining the agendas

Una McNicholl, Family Learning Adviser, Newcastle City Learning

The Newcastle Journey

The Newcastle Family Learning Service, in partnership with the Children's Services' Care to Read Project, has developed provision for foster carers as a discrete group. We want to share our journey in developing this provision and the challenges we faced.

In January 2005, we first engaged a group of six foster carers in a 12-hour Play and Language Course for parents and carers of early years children. We worked with a new partner, the Newcastle Care to Read Project, a project, which provides better access to books for looked-after children. It also seeks to raise expectations of carers to support the literacy and learning of children in their care.

During the initial short course the foster carers provided us with overwhelming evidence of our need to offer further courses. They told us they wanted to be able to support older children with their schoolwork, that they were unfamiliar with the content of the school curriculum, and that they wished to develop their own literacy and numeracy skills. As a result we worked together to engage foster carers in a range of family literacy language and numeracy provision with accreditation opportunities, from workshops to 30-hour courses.

Critical to the success of the programmes has been the working partnership between, and commitment of, the Care to Read Development Worker, the Family Literacy Language and Numeracy Coordinator and family learning tutors.

As well as developing their own literacy and numeracy skills, the carers acquired the skills, knowledge, information and confidence to support the learning and achievement of children in their care and to volunteer to help in school! They all felt these new skills directly impact on the achievement of their children.

The provision: planning, teaching and learning, evaluating

Recruiting a group of eight adults, identifying a central venue accessible to all, and the provision of a crèche when required, due to the fluidity of children's placements with carers, was and will always be a challenge. Our first accredited 30-hour course only recruited four carers. However, we recognised the programme's potential to impact on the educational achievement of looked-after children and its contribution to enhancing the skills and qualifications of carers. We also saw the potential to include these and similar parenting skills programmes as a core part of the foster carer's role and we are quite pleased to see that the government does too, as outlined in their recent Green Paper on looked-after children (DfES, 2006a)!

To improve recruitment on the next courses, we wrote to all foster carers. Participants on prior courses were encouraged to advocate the benefits of the courses. In the summer term 2006 we successfully recruited a group of seven foster carers who completed a 30-hour family literacy course. All the learners progressed to a 30-hour numeracy course the following autumn.

We were very clear about the importance of the characteristics of this group and its dynamics when we were planning the programmes. The group were first and foremost dedicated foster carers. The majority were mature learners over 50, all but one was female and all had been outside formal education for some time.

While the children were from Newcastle, some of the carers lived outside the city. This meant the children attended a variety of different schools in a range of localities, might have been of any age, and were likely to stay with their carers for unpredictable lengths of time. We decided that engaging children on a joint programme with the foster carers on a regular basis was impracticable and we would offer adult-only provision. However, following feedback on the last course, we decided to include a joint activity with children at least once a term, at the weekend.

This approach did hamper our ability to collect data on the impact of the provision on improving the children's learning. However, within their individual learning plans and evaluations the carers documented and identified what they needed to learn in relation to their children's learning and evaluated the impact of this. As one learner said to the Joint Area Review inspector 'this really helped me to help my child through their SATS'.

All courses included full initial and diagnostic assessments, ongoing, interim and end of course assessments, detailed Individual Learning Plans and learner files, and appropriate Skills for Life accreditation. Retention and achievement were excellent and accreditation opportunities ranged from Entry 3 to Level 1 National tests in both literacy and numeracy.

The programmes are flexible enough to incorporate specific needs of the group and their children, for example, a very popular 'Healthy Eating' workshop, facilitated by Newcastle Nutrition. The workshop on how to learn, facilitated by the University of the First Age, was particularly beneficial to carers in understanding how the past experiences of their children may continue to influence how they learn. In other workshops we explored strategies for the engagement of children who present special and challenging needs. We've also been able to support workforce development and progression in foster carers. As well as achieving their initial Skills for Life qualifications, the foster carers intend to progress onto a variety of further education programmes and complete their Level 2 tests. We build an advice and guidance session into each programme.

The future

All partners are fully committed to continuing to offer family learning opportunities for foster carers. The Care to Read Project has ensured the literacy needs of looked after children are considered at a strategic level in Newcastle and we are working pro-actively to address the proposals in the Green Paper. For example, within the foster carers' induction process, we will now promote and encourage foster carers to participate in the courses specially designed for them and the children in their care . We have also been exploring the potential of our Family Finance courses for young people about to leave care and their families.

Cameo 2: Brighton and Hove City Council

Brighton and Hove City Council deliver an OCN-accredited parenting skills programme in partnership with health visitors and family support workers. The course, 'What makes your child tick?' is planned and delivered jointly by a family learning basic skills tutor and a health visitor and/or family support worker, at Children's Centres in Brighton and Hove. Themes covered include stages of child development, the importance of routines and setting loving limits, how children learn and how parents can support them. Classes are a mixture of discussion, small group exercises, quizzes and games, with plenty of opportunities for feedback. There is a clear understanding that parents can have more individual support from health visitors if they require it. Crèche and room hire costs are shared between the services, and each service pays its own teaching costs.

Gill Meyne, Brighton and Hove City Council

Arts and museums: learning can be fun

Loretana Ambrosio, Family Learning Co-ordinator, Peterborough College of Adult Education

We learnt how to create something from a plan, we collected branches from the woods for the tarantula's legs and used tools like a chisel and sandpaper to make them the right size, the course was brilliant!

The provision

Since October 2004, Peterborough College of Adult Education (PCAE) has been running a hands-on creative course for children aged six and above to learn new skills using clay and wood sculpture, along with their parents or carers. We want to demonstrate the positive effect of learning for fun in bringing families together through learning a new skill.

The family sculpture course, forms part of our wider family learning provision. It is funded through our LSC wider family learning budget, with no fees to learners. The course currently runs in the autumn and summer terms, as these are the most popular times.

A highly skilled tutor, who has a wide range of experience in carpentry, clay and wood sculpture, delivers the course. We are fortunate to have access to PCAE's woodwork room which has a wealth of equipment, including workbenches with vices, stores of wood ready to use, pyrography irons, saws, planes, mallets, wood turners and more. However, resources are our challenge, particularly when working away from the college, but we are creative in our use of equipment, for example, we use air-drying clay instead of a kiln.

Children and parents / carers work together on designing projects of their choice. They start by using clay to sculpt something simple. They then research and generate ideas for their main project, by looking through books, magazines etc, and draft a plan together for the project. The projects vary vastly, from animals to bird tables and garden ornaments. Some families will choose to work on several smaller projects rather than one large one. Learning outcomes selected include 'being able to organise the work areas safely', 'use correct personal protective equipment when required' and 'being able to select appropriate tools for tasks.'

Selecting materials to work with sometimes depends on the age of the child. Older children tend to select wood, which involves using a lot more tools and equipment. Younger children usually focus on using clay or pyrography irons. Families tend to become very involved in and particular about their work, so projects often take several weeks. The tutor includes elements of health and safety in every session.

Planning, progression and quality

The family learning co-ordinator and course tutor liaise at all stages of the planning and delivery of the course. The marketing manager undertakes the course publicity, which includes sending posters to local schools, advertising in community venues such as libraries and children's centres. We recently advertised in the local newspaper, which received a good response from a wider audience. The course has attracted the attention of the local media, and we have had a spread in the local newspaper. Publicity is one of the areas that we would like to develop in the future, thereby reaching more families.

Family sculpture is one of the more innovative and creative courses within our wider family learning curriculum. It attracts new families into family learning and leads on to further learning. From this course, families access other family learning courses, and adults progress onto other creative courses such as woodwork, pottery, art or upholstery. Our Management Information Systems run an annual report to track which of the adult learners enrol on other courses at PCAE. We also aim to track what learners plan to do before they complete their course, by detailing this in their learning plans.

Learners can access information about further learning through our college customer service staff. The tutor is also able to offer information, advice and support. The tutor's inclusive teaching style takes into account the level of ability and progress of each family, and our learner support co-ordinator contacts individuals who have disclosed a disability, before the start of the course to see how best we can support their needs.

We use Individual Learning Plans to measure achievement of learning outcomes, which vary for different families and different projects. A one-adult-one-child family enthuses:

We have all learned many new skills, all staff involved have been very positive and supportive. The tutor was excellent, always willing to share, help with ideas and solve problems. We had a brilliant time and made new friends.

We have changed and developed the course over the period that we have been running it. For example, shortening the duration of the course has improved retention, and embedding the RARPA process has helped us to evidence achievements through the use of photographs.

Cameo 3: Camden Adult and Community Learning Service

'Families in the Frame' is a family learning art project provided in four venues in the London Borough of Camden. Developed through a partnership of Camden's Adult and Community Learning Service, City Lit, the Foundling Museum and the National Portrait Gallery, the project is taught by an art tutor and a family learning tutor working together. Family participants develop their understanding of portraiture and their art skills through making a portrait of a family member from recycled newspapers and magazines. They visit the National Portrait Gallery in order to learn more about exhibiting work, and their finished work is exhibited in the gallery space at the Foundling Museum.

The project allows families to explore and celebrate relationships and to reflect on the characters of their family members. It also gives families, many of whom have never visited a museum, an opportunity to discover what galleries and museums have to offer, and that many are a free resource offering a fun and educational day out for families. Staff from the museum, gallery, college, schools and learning centres also have an opportunity to learn from working with each other.

Jennie Lavis, Camden Adult and Community Learning Service

Cameo 4: Birmingham Adult Education Service

The 'Family Playmakers Project' in Birmingham provides an innovative way of providing a 'Play and Language Course' in early years settings. The project, offered in five locations, involves 2–3 year-olds and their parents in a creative approach to developing a script for a play. Children and parents contribute ideas and thoughts for the content of a play, which is then written by the project's theatre worker and performed at the Birmingham Repertory theatre by professional actors. The project enhances the communication, language and literacy skills of parents and children, as well as giving them access to the rich experience of the theatre.

Beryl Bateson, Birmingham Adult Education Service

Cameo 5: Richmond upon Thames Family Learning and Orleans House Gallery

Richmond upon Thames Family Learning, in partnership with the Orleans House Gallery, used a course of discussion and drawing-based sessions to enable families to become involved in the local planning and implementation of *Every Child Matters*. A professional artist and gallery staff worked with the participation co-ordinator for Richmond to deliver 'Every Drawing Matters' in 2005–06. The role of the participation co-ordinator is to consult with local children regarding their needs, and this project provided an innovative way of consulting, while also contributing to the *Every Child Matters* outcomes in its own right.

The programme focused on illustrating the objectives of *Every Child Matters*, using the five key outcomes as a starting point. The drawings created by the children and their families were displayed in an exhibition at Orleans House Gallery and launched the new Education and Children's Services department in April 2006. The process of creating the drawings helped to develop visual literacy skills and verbal communication skills, encouraging parents and their children to share and discuss opinions. It also helped to develop an understanding of how the children and families could make a positive contribution to their local community. The exhibition of the drawings shared the issues explored with the wider community.

Alexandra Bennett, London Borough of Richmond upon Thames

Family reading and libraries: reading together

Wendy Bond, Learning Manager, Lincolnshire County Council Libraries and Learning Service

Changing the culture

Lincolnshire County Council Libraries and Learning Service and partners work to encourage men in Lincoln Prison to maintain links with their children, grandchildren or step-children through reading and sharing books. Here we give a flavour of how the 'Reading Together' project brings benefits to very vulnerable and excluded families.

HMP Lincoln is a category B closed prison with restrictions on visiting rights, making it difficult for children to keep in touch with their fathers. Recently, the Governor and senior management have committed themselves to improving provision for prisoners' families. This has included forming a Kids VIP group in the prison, refurbishing the children's area for visits, overcoming the resistance of some prison staff to the idea of including prisoners' families in their work remit, and addressing communication difficulties between uniformed and non-uniformed staff.

The Reading Together project, which began in 2005 with funding from the Paul Hamlyn Foundation, is playing an instrumental role in these changes. In particular, by showing that interaction between prison staff and families is possible, we have helped the prison to develop new protocols to make the visits work.

As the two-year funding comes to an end, we intend to mainstream this project in the newly formed Libraries and Learning service, contributing to our remit of providing services to those parts of the community most in need.

Reading Together: how it works

Prisoners choose books from a Reading Together collection in the prison library, to work on with their children. While duplicate copies of the chosen books are sent to families' local libraries, we make contact with the families and help them to join their local library and access the books that dad has chosen for them.

Dad and children exchange letters about the books, with ideas and help from the prison's Writer in Residence and the project staff. Once they have shared three books, the children receive a goody bag of books, tapes and activities, and are allowed to visit to engage in storytelling and reading-related activities in the prison visits area.

Before we get to this stage, a lot of work is needed with the prisoners and their partners or ex-partners. Many of the prisoners are not comfortable with reading and writing, and some of the mums and carers have severe literacy problems themselves, and don't feel confident to walk into the library and enrol their children.

We hold informal weekly sessions with dads, based on the foundation stage curriculum and the National Literacy Strategy. We interview them individually and discuss their literacy level. If they require help, we put measures in place to support them so that they can successfully achieve the project aims. We use creative writing, story-telling and drama to encourage the men and their families to venture into reading and writing. The men also learn about how children learn to read and write, and how parents can support this process.

We encourage the men to contact their partners themselves. We then follow up with a letter and a phone call. Some partners don't want to respond, because their relationship with the prisoner is irreparably damaged. For others, although they are willing, they find it difficult to offer the high level of commitment and motivation needed, because of problems in their own lives. We offer support and encouragement to the mums, and try to make it as easy for them as possible, for example by facilitating contact with their local library. For those families where the partner doesn't want regular contact, we offer dads an opportunity to do a Storybook Dad CD.

The children get a Kids' Pack, which includes their library card, felt pens or crayons, ideas sheets for writing to dad, and badges and stickers. The children get excited when the Kids' Packs arrive in the post, and they often persuade mum to take them to the library. For very young children and babies, mums and carers are encouraged to describe their reactions and to let the dads know what stage the children are at. The parents are encouraged to have a dialogue about the children's development.

Progress is measured using generic learning outcomes and also includes user feedback and consultation. The project was evaluated by the Paul Hamlyn Foundation after the first year. We made some changes in response to the evaluation's findings, including simplifying the library-joining procedure and breaking down the reward system into smaller steps.

The project has reached 67 families over the past 18 months. The evaluation and feedback show that the project has been instrumental in improving prisoners' relationships with their families, a key factor in reducing recidivism, and in helping families support their children's formal learning,

> *Since coming to the Reading Together project I've had a good relationship with my son. It's educational for him because we do games for him to learn off. Also it's improving his reading…*

> *It has helped us understand more about kids reading.*

Many of the families participating in this project are at risk in some way and are often stigmatised and marginalised because they have a family member in prison. Reading Together helps to integrate the families into community life through participation in library-based activities. Using the library also brings them into contact with a wealth of services available to assist them in gaining access to learning and work, for example free internet access. Their engagement with the local library often continues when the dads are released:

We go to the book group in the library every Tuesday now.

Cameo 6: Adult Education Cumbria

'Story sacks with dads at Haverigg Prison' is a joint initiative between Family Learning Adult Education Cumbria, and Cumbria Library Service. As well as enhancing the skills of dads and male carers in prison, it helps to keep the much-needed contact between male prisoners and their children, a factor which has been identified as helping towards reduced re-offending and successful resettlement on release. Reading stories to children is not a role that some dads traditionally recognise as theirs. Often it is seen as the job of teachers or mums. The men therefore need to learn the new skills of story-telling, being creative in presenting the stories to their children, developing strategies for working with their children to enhance learning and development. After five learning sessions in the prison library to help them develop these skills, the men produce a CD for their children in the prison IT workshop. The CD contains their reading of the story with added sound effects and voice simulation, as well as a personal message to their children. As one prisoner commented:

More of these courses should be put on for people as things like this will help people realise what kids are all about ...Things like this really do help people bring up their children in the right manner.

Sue Doyle, Family Learning, Adult Education Cumbria

Family languages: sharing experiences

Karen Fairfax-Cholmeley, Formerly Family Literacy Language and Numeracy Manager, Oxfordshire County Council Social and Community Services

Engaging Pakistani parents

Oxfordshire has a growing number of children of Pakistani heritage in its schools. Raising the achievement of these children is one of the outcomes of the Joint Area Review. For us, and the partners in this programme, involving parents and carers in their children's learning is key to raising their achievement.

The course was initiated by the Head of Comper Foundation Stage School. She was concerned at the difficulties some of the cultural minority children were having in settling into class and was very anxious to engage the parents in some way. Together we devised a 'Keeping up with the Children' programme, recognising that to run a course successfully for families not traditionally engaged in learning takes a long time. After a shaky start, by September 2006, the course began to develop a life of its own.

The learners wanted to be more involved in the school and local community and they wanted to share their experiences of being Pakistani Muslim women living in Oxford. They decided to write a booklet together, reflecting their lives and experiences and to present the booklet to the school for sharing with staff, children and other parents. In this way the concept of 'Keeping up with the Children' became a two-way exchange. It provided not just for the parents and carers gaining more insight into the learning that was taking place at school, but school staff and other families gained an insight into the lives of children and families from the Pakistani community.

Delivering the provision

The course is a customised version of the 20-hour 'Keeping up with the Children' model. The women meet for two hours a week at the school, sharing their experiences through writing the booklet, finding out about how their children learn in the Foundation stage and how they can support them, whilst working on their own English language skills. The course is double staffed with an adult FLLN tutor with ESOL qualifications, and a bilingual support worker who is also a nursery nurse in the School.

The children, aged from 18 months to 5 years old, are involved in some of the sessions. Activities are set up to be inclusive across the age range, with the children participating at their individual stages of development. For example, when sharing a story, very young children enjoy the interaction with 'their' adult, those who are slightly older enjoy the pictures and predicting the story, whilst the oldest children start following the text and picking out words.

The first part of each session reflects the way children learn in the Foundation stage. The session starts with a joint circle time with songs and rhymes, from English and Pakistani cultures, followed by shared news. Children's storybooks, selected from the school, form the basis for English language work. Activities mirror those used in class, such as storytelling with story sacks, retelling stories, playing and making games. On some occasions, the children join the session for the story and activities.

The second part of the session is devoted to planning and writing the booklet. Learners practise their English oral skills through interviewing each other about their experiences in Britain and Pakistan and their aspirations for the future. Practical activities include deciding on layout and illustrations, making a related game, looking at maps, drawing family trees and analysing their daily routines.

English language levels in the class range from emerging Entry 1 to Entry 3 so teaching is differentiated. The bilingual support ensures that everyone is able to contribute fully and understand the rationale behind the activities.

Assessment at the beginning of the course relates to the outcomes identified on the learners' individual learning programmes (ILPs). It involves some oral work and reading and writing on topics connected with the children, for example reading a page from a children's book. Learning is checked regularly through tutor feedback on tasks and weekly oral evaluations at the end of sessions, which are recorded on the ILPs. Children's achievement and progress are noted through observation by the class teachers.

Several factors have contributed to the programme's success. Firstly, the learners had a story they wanted to tell and were enthusiastic and motivated, resulting in a rich and fruitful interchange of ideas and information.

The enthusiasm and expertise of the two staff on the project were also vital. The adult tutor enabled the learners' aims to be woven into a 'Keeping up with the Children' course. The willingness of both staff to listen, prompt and value the learners' contributions, ensured that the course responded to the needs and interests of the learners. The involvement of the school in planning and evaluating the sessions was also vital to this responsive process, as was their support and positive attitude towards parental involvement.

Finally, the recognition that aunts and grandmothers also play an important part in bringing up the children and should be involved in the learning, helped towards the programme's 100 per cent retention and achievement rate, as learners felt more confident coming to class with a relative.

The programme resulted in families making a positive contribution to the school, by being more involved in school life. The head teacher felt that the fact that the families were enjoying being in school more made it easier to involve them in the school's activities.

The adults have become more aware of how their children learn, which it is anticipated will result in increased achievement for the children. One learner said:

> *We've learnt how they learn in Nursery – how they play, it's good. Before [the course] we didn't know and now we know about what the children do and we can do it too.*

All the adults were keen to continue learning English, and some are seeing how this might improve their economic well-being. For example, one learner who married young and had six children, now wants to improve her English and to go on to study medicine. As the local ESOL classes, to which the learners might have progressed, are already over-subscribed, we are planning to offer the ESOL Trinity qualification on FLLN courses at Comper School.

Cameo 7: Somerset County Council Family Learning

Somerset has found that the need for FLLN ESOL provision has increased over recent years, with a growth in the number of foreign nationals attracted to the area for employment, with their children attending local schools. The County Council's FLLN team work with local schools to deliver 40-hour 'Step Ahead' courses. These courses provide a structured scheme of work with equal emphasis on the skills of reading, writing, speaking and listening, but with different interlocking themes for each. As well as preparing parents for progression to a structured ESOL programme, the course encourages families to learn together and works towards integration and an understanding of school procedures.

Margaret Luck, Somerset County Council Family Learning

Cameo 8: Croydon Continuing Education and Training (CETS)

CETS works with LEaF House, a charity located in a council estate in Croydon, with high levels of poverty and deprivation. The charity provides family support, including drop-ins and toddler groups, basic skills and ICT classes and skills check, as well as advice on various issues such as housing. CETS delivered two Early Start literacy courses at the centre, during 2006, for parents/carers of children aged 0–3 years, all of whom were recruited from the toddler group and drop-in.

Most of the group was white British; however, it included three ESOL learners, one of whom was a grandmother from Sri Lanka who cared for her granddaughter part-time. The group started with the introductory course and then progressed on to a longer 30-hour course. The course focused on integrated work on learners' own literacy skills with ideas and activities based around supporting their children. The majority of the parents completed and passed an OCN accreditation, 'Supporting Children's Language Development'. One of the ESOL learners went on to do a child-care course at Croydon College.

Musseret Anwar, Croydon Continuing Education and Training (CETS)

Section 4
EVERY CHILD MATTERS
THEMED CASE STUDIES

This section shares case studies and smaller 'cameos' demonstrating how family learning contributes directly to the Every Child Matters outcomes.

Be healthy

Be healthy

The '*Every Child Matters*' outcomes framework defines 'Be healthy' in the following ways:

- Physically healthy
- Mentally and emotionally healthy
- Sexually healthy
- Healthy lifestyles
- Choose not to take illegal drugs
- Parents, carers and families promote healthy choices

Introduction to 'Be Healthy'

Penny Lamb

In the field of family learning, we have always tried to join up agendas and to use a holistic approach in our work with families. The *Every Child Matters* agenda gives us the opportunity to consolidate this way of working: to think 'outside the box', where 'the box' represents the artificial divisions between adult learning and children's learning; school learning and home learning; and between activities in the community and activities at work.

Nowhere is this more obvious than in thinking about the key theme of 'Be Healthy'. It feels as if we are constantly bombarded with stories that seem to heap guilt and blame onto parents and carers: childhood obesity, unhealthy eating, school dinners, lack of exercise, mental health problems, the impact on children when families do not spend time together. Is it any wonder that parents and carers often feel uneasy and lack confidence as they interact with schools and with health and social care professionals? And yet, we know that healthy, happy families nurture strong active citizens for the present and the future.

Through family learning activities, we can use a positive approach to supporting families in their physical, emotional and social well-being. Family learning works jointly with schools, NHS Primary Care Trusts, libraries and many other partners, supporting families to adopt healthier lifestyles, to eat and drink well, to stay safe, while helping to enhance their self-esteem. There are many exciting and imaginative family learning activities that share an understanding of improving health, not only within families, but between families and between communities, crossing cultural divides. For example, approaches to sharing healthy cuisines across cultures help to enhance community cohesion.

However, it is not always about the new and the innovative: the joy of a parent and child sharing a book together, particularly one that they have made themselves, or learning how to share stories and rhymes: these are activities that have been with us for a long time. Perhaps, we need to re-consider these programmes in the light of the *Every Child Matters* agenda and look at the learning elements for both parents and children, in terms of their impact on health and social well-being.

The following case study from Stockton-on-Tees, and the cameos from York and Sunderland, show how family learning can help to influence both physical and emotional health. They also highlight the contribution that family learning can make to help partner organisations meet their objectives and targets. For example, The Stockton project works with Stockton Healthy Schools, part of the National Healthy Schools programme, a partnership between the health service and schools, that aims, among other things, to support children and young people in developing healthy behaviour. The Healthy Schools Standard focuses particularly on the areas of Personal, Social and Health Education, healthy eating, physical activity and emotional health/well-being.

The Stockton project was part-funded by the local PCT, because it helped them meet their objectives in promoting the 5-a-day campaign. However, family learning programmes such as the examples given here, can also be mapped to some of the standards of the National Service Framework (NSF) for Children, Young People and Maternity Services.

Be healthy: Reaching out for health

Ann Walker, Family Learning Subject Leader, Stockton Adult Education Service

Meeting local needs

Stockton Adult Education Service's family learning team delivered the 'Being Healthy' programme in 2005–06, in partnership with the Local Primary Care Trust (PCT), the 'Write to Read' regeneration project and 'Stockton Healthy Schools'. We developed the programme in response to a number of converging needs: research from 'Write to Read' identifying healthy eating as a local health priority; the '5-a-day' campaign by the PCT; requests from headteachers for a course that would help parents to manage their children's behaviour; requests from parents wanting to find out about particular developments in schools; ideas from tutors; and the changing national agenda, including *Every Child Matters*.

Our aims for the project were to promote healthy eating and raise awareness of the 'whole person' approach to health. We had started with a healthy eating project at a primary school, working with the PCT during the 'five-a-day' campaign. At the same time, we were receiving requests from headteachers who were experiencing problems in the classroom caused by the disruptive behaviour of increasing numbers of children of all ages and backgrounds. They wanted a course that would help parents teach their children how to empathise, set rules and boundaries at home and cope with anger. We identified that family learning could help families to develop a 'whole person' approach to health, through a two-strand approach.

The first strand is a two-hour healthy eating workshop, based on the book *Oliver's Vegetables* by Vivian French. This is delivered by our outreach team as a one-off stand-alone session. As well as delivering it in schools, we have been able to work with the transient population in a variety of locations, including the Women's Refuge and travellers from Yarm Fair at the town's library. For many of these learners, a commitment of even six sessions would not have been possible. This format has offered us a way of taking family learning out into the community to work with the widest diversity of groups.

The second strand of the project is designed as a follow-on from the workshop. Using the 'Keeping up with the Children' format, we developed a series of activities, including 'Social and Emotional Education of the Child', which offers parents a range of skills to enable them to support their child's healthy development.

Delivering the programme

We chose the book *Oliver's Vegetables* as the basis for the workshop sessions, because it tells the story of a boy who ate only chips but learned to like vegetables after spending time in his grandpa's garden. We developed a series of activities around this story, including designing and describing cartoon food characters, and recognising fruits and vegetables. Parents and children make stick puppets together to extend the story, and the session closes with fruit tasting. The participants then receive a copy of *The Fantastic Fun Filled Recipe Book,* funded by the PCT.

All the workshop activities are mapped to the Core Curriculum and to the *Every Child Matters* Outcomes Framework, namely 'Be healthy', 'Enjoy and achieve' and 'Make a positive contribution'. We have found that the activities have particularly helped to extend speaking and listening skills (currently high profile in Foundation Stage), as parents and children work closely together. The fruit character tasks also help to develop literacy skills.

We were already running 'Keeping up with the Children' courses, but we saw the opportunity to incorporate extra elements that would contribute to the 'whole person' approach to health and learning. These include social and emotional education, which takes place towards the end of the course. This includes anger management, calming techniques and healthy eating; offering parents a range of skills to enable them to support their child, as well as through their schoolwork. Discussions on social and emotional learning have allowed parents to support each other by airing their own concerns and experiences, which in turn helps to increase their confidence and parenting skills.

We are continuing to develop the 'Being healthy' element of the 'Keeping Up With the Children' courses, and the good practice that the tutors have built up during the project has strengthened our delivery of these classes. The workshop format has proved so successful that we are using it with other books, and to meet other priorities.

As with all our courses, we ensure that students have access to a high quality Information, Advice and Guidance (IAG) service. Our IAG service is Matrix-accredited, and the outreach team who deliver the workshop also hold IAG qualifications at Level 3. This, coupled with a wide experience of family learning, enables them to guide learners not only to the most appropriate family learning course for them, but to consider a wider range of options. During the six week 'Keeping up with the Children' course, the tutor regularly uses her own knowledge of family learning courses to guide the group when they ask 'what can we do next?' Students have moved on to courses such as ICT, and 'Art and Craft Together'.

Managing the programme

Our Family Learning Curriculum Plan highlights the importance of working with partners and projects to extend capacity and maximise potential for all parties. This project effectively combined the resources and expertise of a range of partners – the Write to Read project, North Tees PCT, the local LSC (who provide the bulk of the funding) and Stockton Healthy Schools. As it is a relatively small-scale project, our Family Learning Curriculum Manager is closely involved in operational and strategic management at all stages. The project is monitored at monthly team meetings and via our management information system.

Neither of the programmes is accredited but, for the 'Keeping up with the Children' course, we use a specially designed booklet as an Individual Learning Plan for recognising and recording progress and achievement. This establishes both long and short-term targets for the learners, which we review regularly. At the end of the course, learners complete the 'what next' section to provide information on planned progression. We also ask them to identify any additional benefits gained from the course, such as improved confidence, so that we can record 'soft' outcomes.

We have learned that we need to agree a timetable for publicity with the venue, so that parents and carers have plenty of notice and can make arrangements to attend the programme or workshop.

Across the two strands of the programme, we have so far worked with 143 children and 153 adults, with 100 per cent retention and achievement. The most common comment on evaluation forms is how much learners have enjoyed spending time with their children. The word 'fun' is used a lot!

Cameo 8: York Family Learning Service

'Fun with Family Cooking' is for families identified as needing additional support. Each week, parents or carers spend three hours preparing and sharing a meal with their children, while at the same time, improving their literacy skills. By the end of the 32 weeks, parents achieve their Entry Level accreditation in literacy as well as producing a cookbook. They all leave with ideas and knowledge to improve their children's eating habits, and most progress to further family learning literacy courses. We run this programme in partnership with SureStart.

Lorna Batten, York Family Learning Service

Cameo 9: Sunderland Family Adult and Community Learning

Family Football Coaching courses encourage families to spend more time involved in physical activities, whilst also persuading men to take a more active role in their children's education. The courses are based around football, and are run by the Foundation of the local football club, Sunderland AFC. This acts as a hook to encourage participation.

Parents and carers who have taken part find that they spend more time with their children in activities such as walking and cycling. Some parents and carers even go on to help run community football teams. They also learn about the emotional needs of children, safe exercise and health eating, as well as learning styles and the national curriculum.

During the 10-week programme, parents and children learn together, develop their communication skills and motivate each other to improve levels of skills and fitness. The courses are held in schools and community settings, during the day, evenings and weekends, particularly in areas of high deprivation where many families do not access other learning opportunities.

The Club works in partnership with Sunderland Adult and Community Learning, Sunderland Wellness Centres and other local authority initiatives to improve health, fitness and well-being.

Maggie Smith, Sunderland Family Adult and Community Learning

Stay safe

Stay Safe

The 'Stay safe' outcome of '*Every Child Matters*' encompasses a wide definition of safety, including:

- Being safe from maltreatment, neglect, violence and sexual exploitation
- Being safe from accidental injury and death
- Being safe from bullying and discrimination
- Being safe from crime and anti-social behaviour in and out of school
- Having security, stability and being cared for
- Parents, carers and families providing safe homes and stability

Introduction to 'Stay safe'

Clare Meade, NIACE

The safety and welfare of all children is at the centre of the *'Every Child Matters: change for children'* programme which followed the high profile inquiry (Laming, 2003) into the death of Victoria Climbie in 2000, and the Joint Chief Inspectors' Report on Safeguarding Children (Department of Health, 2002).

It was acknowledged that even simple changes can make a big difference to children's lives, and that all agencies and their staff need to work together in order to make the best use of specialist skills, and to ensure that the child and their experience is the centre of attention.

A key message of the reforms is the importance of services and agencies continuing to move towards prevention and early intervention. Valuing the input of parents and carers as partners at every stage, and engaging families, are also recognised as vital if reforms are to be effective.

Partnership work is a major strength of family learning programmes. Family learning providers work with a wide range of organisations including health, social care, museums and voluntary organisations, to develop and provide programmes that engage parents and carers in a range of settings.

Family learning takes learning to where parents and carers are located. Programmes are run in many settings, including children's centres, extended schools, health centres, libraries and community centres. They provide opportunities to develop a curriculum that meets the needs of families in different settings and on a range of topics, working collaboratively and drawing on the expertise of other professionals. Activities look positively at how families can address some of the issues around 'staying safe', for example challenging bullying, substance/alcohol abuse and antisocial behaviour.

An example of this is highlighted in the case study from the Isle of Wight where they have developed a programme on law and order, working with the Youth Offending Service, magistrates, police and the prison service to give families an insight into the legal system. This programme correlates well with the increasingly co-operative working style being required of agencies involved in both children's services and youth offending, working to Local Authority Children's and Young People's Plans (CYPPs) and Youth Justice Plans. There can be a role for family learning in helping to implement these plans, as there can be in Safer School Partnerships, which aim to tackle crime and anti-social behaviour in schools.

Other examples where family learning can contribute to 'Stay Safe' include activities around exploring the local area, discussions on road safety and personal safety, looking at safe environments and identifying hazards in the home.

Stay Safe: An introduction to law and order

Sarah Teague, Family Learning Manager, Isle of Wight Council

A little wiser and more aware of our responsibility to help educate all of our children to avoid the world of crime, we went back to our families and homes.

The right people in the right place at the right time

All of the Isle of Wight's family learning programmes are mapped to the ECM five outcomes. 'Law and Order: an introduction for families', introduced in 2001, is an OCN-accredited Level 1 course that supports the aim for children and young people to be 'safe from crime and anti-social behaviour in and out of school' and to 'have security, stability and be cared for.' It looks at local crime, how young people get involved in anti-social behaviour, the stages of the youth justice system and what it means for families.

At our school-based Family Learning Centre, we hold termly coffee mornings, and it was at one of these coffee mornings that the idea for this course began to develop. Mothers were discussing how they wanted to know more about the judicial system before their children got into trouble. One parent in particular was very keen to move this idea forward, and she was instrumental in getting other parents involved. She worked with the tutor to write the documentation for the Open College Network panel to accredit the course, and the accreditation was a personal as well as a service achievement, particularly as it was our first accredited course.

We recognised that getting specialist partners involved from the outset would be key, and we were lucky that one of our tutors was also involved in youth offending work, so knew who to contact. The partners provide speakers for the sessions, and these speakers have committed to three courses a year voluntarily - they have found that they learn as much from the experience as the parents do.

Running the course

The course offers a progression from initial wider family learning. It is aimed at parents and carers primarily, but the learners share their experiences with their families, and have informed discussions at home about the issues raised. Interestingly, before we got accreditation for the course, it recruited mothers exclusively. However, once we had gained OCN accreditation men became interested, and it now attracts men and women in equal numbers.

The course has a recommended 30-hour delivery time over 10 weeks. During this period, participants receive a variety of presentations, and the course facilitator ensures that the links between speakers are clear to the learners. The facilitator is key both in terms of co-ordination and in dealing with issues that may arise during the sessions, where a link with family support workers is also vital.

We aim to make the course as interactive as possible. For example, during one session the magistrate sets up a mock court, which leads to a discussion on the court system. This is followed by a visit to the local County Court to observe a morning's proceedings. The youth offending team discuss roles and responsibilities with parents, using a quiz based on ages and stages of responsibility, from 'The legal age for babysitting – is there one?' to 'Can a parent be prosecuted for disposing of drugs found in their child's room?' Parents and carers are encouraged to take this quiz home and try it out on members of the family to stimulate discussion in the home.

A session from the head of the Board of Visitors led to a prison visit being included in the programme. This visit has an impact on both offenders and learners alike. The offenders are very interested in the reasons for the parents' visit and are very positive about the effect an interested parent would have had on their behaviour when they were children.

For the learners, the prison visit is often the highlight of the course. It generates debate and challenges some preconceptions. This has led to interesting discussions on stereotyping that have to be sensitively and thoroughly discussed with the professional speakers. The prison visit has a profound impact on the learners, and their feelings are communicated to family and peers alike through completion of their weekly learner diary.

One of a variety of methods we use to gather evidence of progress and achievement is a reflective learner diary. The learner completes an evaluation at the end of each session stating what they already knew before the session and noting what was the most important piece of information that they learned that session. We undertake course evaluation with learners to find out how discussions have been influenced at home by the course, and we ask the learners to evaluate the impact they think the course will have on their families. Achievement and retention rates are very high, with 96 per cent retention and, of those who completed, 100 per cent achieving accreditation.

As well as contributing towards the ECM outcomes for their children, we also aim to help the adults to progress to further learning. To this end, we have a qualified Information, Advice and Guidance worker within the team who has created a specialist IAG pack for the course, highlighting possible careers or volunteering opportunities that learners may be interested in.

Two learners from the first group undertook training to become prison visitors; one went on to study for a GCSE in Law at the local FE College, and two applied to be on the Youth Justice Board. Most learners have gone on to further learning. We have also responded to learners' requests to take the course at a higher level, and to learn more about drugs and their misuse. We are developing a Level 2 law and order course, and are planning a supplementary level one about drugs misuse and sexual health. We will soon be able to offer a portfolio of courses to support the Stay Safe outcome of *Every Child Matters*.

Managing the course

We have a very robust quality improvement system that runs through office files, staff files, meeting minutes and computer files organisation. In practice, this means that every action we undertake 'fits' into an organised system. Although this may sound restrictive, it is truly a vital tool in our work and we adapt the system constantly to take account of new initiatives and areas of work. As manager of the service I would say that adopting a quality framework has been a hugely significant factor in our success.

We hold the Matrix Quality mark for our Information, Advice and Guidance Service and I would wholeheartedly recommend services working towards this accreditation. As always, it is the process that is so worthwhile, ensuring all staff understand the service and are able to influence it and drive it forward.

During the last two years we have introduced a course review system which helps the team to analyse what works with a course and what does not, in order to make changes for the next course.

We have learned that developing a curriculum involving so many partners can be very time-consuming and a lengthy process. We have encountered all the highs and lows of partnership working and it has taken a period of about five years to develop the course fully.

We have also found that, whilst the prison visit has a profound effect on learners, it does limit the number of learners and can be difficult to arrange. In future, we are hoping to link with the 'Prison? Me? No Way!' project run in schools, and perhaps to arrange prison visits in conjunction with them.

We would say to other providers that developing a curriculum from suggestions by parents and carers about their needs is the most successful method. Something that you think might work is an innovation, and a calculated risk is a pilot!

Cameo 10: Lancashire Adult Learning

Having recently developed a partnership with the Council's Road Safety team, Lancashire Adult Learning is in the first stages of developing a 'Staying Safe' programme for parents and carers. It is envisaged that the programme will link 'Road Safety', 'First Aid', 'Save a Child's Life' and 'Safe Use of the Internet', and will provide a progression opportunity for parents to become volunteers delivering the road safety message to children. The project will combine the Adult Learning Service's expertise in engaging parents and carers, with the Road Safety team's knowledge of safety issues. It will be funded by the LSC and the Road Safety Group.

Mandy Williams, Lancashire Adult Learning

Cameo 11: Swindon Learning Partnership

Swindon Learning Partnership runs 'Family Health and Safety' as part of its wider family learning programme called SOKs (Supporting our Kids) Clubs in primary schools, children's centres and family centres in neighbourhood renewal areas of Swindon. The programme enables parents and carers to complete fun activities with their children that promote healthy and safe lifestyles. Activities include identifying possible hazards in the home, learning some emergency first aid procedures, visits from Fire Safety Officers, Road Safety Officers, School nurses and drugs workers. Learners can progress on to accredited First Aid and Early Years certificated courses.

Jackie Crowther, Swindon Learning Partnership

Enjoy and achieve

The *Every Child Matters* framework defines 'Enjoy and achieve' in the following ways:

- Being ready for school
- Attending and enjoying school
- Achieving stretching national educational standards at primary school
- Achieving personal and social development and enjoying recreation
- Achieving stretching national educational standards at secondary school
- Parents, carers and families supporting learning

Introduction to 'Enjoy and achieve'

Keith McDowall, Knowsley Family and Community Education

Every Child Matters seeks to ensure that children achieve high educational standards, enjoy education and through it achieve personal and social development. Family learning has a unique and essential contribution to make to the achievement of this aim, recognising as it does that children's families are an even more important context for and influence on their learning and development than schools.

Underpinning all family learning is the notion that the most successful learning takes place where family members engage in learning together, supporting and encouraging each other's learning and having opportunities to achieve as individuals. Sessions enable parents to take part in learning together with their children and to extend and develop this learning partnership at home and in the wider world. Parents gain a better understanding of how children learn and are taught in schools and how they can support their children's learning and development. Through developing parents' own skills, confidence and achievement, family learning enables and encourages them to fully contribute to their children's education and to work in partnership with schools. Children take pride in their parents' contributions and achievements and are helped to see education as a part of their family and community life, something that they can have ownership of.

Perhaps most importantly, family learning enables children and adults to enjoy learning and have fun whilst they learn together, as anyone who has participated in family learning, talked to family learners, or who has seen parents' records and descriptions of learning activities that they have done with their children, will roundly endorse.

Family learning is not only based on learning in partnership, but also operates through partnership working between local authorities, schools, adult education, SureStart, children's centres and the voluntary sector, to name but a few!. *Every Child Matters* will provide increasing incentives and opportunities to create new partnerships to deliver family learning and through the flexibility and adaptability of the family learning approach, to engage new groups, enabling them to take advantage of its unique support tailored to their specific needs, to enjoy learning and to begin to achieve their true potential.

The Juskidz case study shows one way in which family learning can help parents and carers to support the learning of their child, while also helping children to develop personally and socially and enjoy recreation. The other examples in this section also help towards these aims, as well as helping young children be ready for school and school-age children to enjoy school.

Family learning programmes that contribute to the 'Enjoy and achieve' outcome may also contribute to other local and national strategies, such as local authorities' local play strategies and the DfES 'Learning outside the classroom' strategy.

Enjoy and achieve: Juskidz

Keith McDowall, Family Learning Manager, Knowsley Family and Community Education (FACE)

Space for carers

At Knowsley FACE Family Learning, as well as offering universal provision, with opportunities for all parents to engage further in supporting their children's education and developing their own skills, we also provide a growing range of targeted family learning programmes. These are designed to meet the needs of specific groups who may be under-represented in learning, or who have a particularly high degree of need for support.

The project we want to talk about here is one of these targeted programmes. The project was set up in partnership with 'Juskidz', a self-help group providing respite and support to parents and carers of children with physical disabilities and/or learning difficulties and is specifically designed to enable them to participate in family learning. It is based in Tower Hill, an area of high socio-economic deprivation in Knowsley.

The 'Juskidz' family learning project provides parents, whose daily lives are largely taken up with caring for their children, with some space for their own development. As well as supporting the parents/carers in learning and in improving their skills and confidence, the project also empowers them to help their children enjoy and achieve their full potential, and provides a stimulating and enjoyable recreational experience for the children.

The 'Juskidz' group initiated the project. They were pro-actively seeking new avenues and partnerships that would help them and their group develop. For us at the family learning team, this presented an invaluable opportunity to support a group of parents who, because of their caring responsibilities, would find it difficult to access many forms of learning. We recognised that a family learning course specifically tailored to their needs could be hugely beneficial for both parents and children. The programme not only enables the parents to explore their own personal development; it enhances the experience of, and celebrates the participation of, young people with a variety of physical and learning difficulties.

Sharing the planning

We plan the curriculum with the group on an ongoing (usually termly) basis so that it is relevant to their needs and interests, and provides challenge and opportunities for progression. This has been a learning process for both the 'Juskidz' group and for us, and the process has taken time to become effective. The initial curriculum focused on preparing learners to take the national literacy and numeracy tests. However, it became apparent over time that an embedded approach to literacy and numeracy provided a more effective starting point for the group. Level 1 Open College accreditation, together with our RARPA process, offer 'Juskidz' learners the opportunity to achieve and to progress on to more formal qualifications.

The current curriculum centres on personal and social development, including: making choices and decisions; developing self-confidence; assertiveness; dealing with stress; organisation and time-management. The tutor has created a website for the group, which includes a facility for accessing course information and materials on-line. Within the programme of weekly two-hour Saturday sessions, there are also opportunities for 'one-off' sessions led by guest speakers. For example, a member of Knowsley's Healthy Schools team led a recent session focusing on healthy eating.

At registration, we invite the learners to identify and discuss their learning needs with the course tutor. They also undertake an initial screening and self-assessment to help identify their literacy/numeracy needs and complete an individual learning plan. This supplies detailed information about learners' individual needs, which enables the course tutor to offer an ongoing high level of individual support to learners during sessions. The tutor is also supported by a Classroom Assistant who provides additional one-to-one support for individual learners.

While the parents/carers take part in structured sessions, led by a qualified adult education tutor, their children take part in less structured sessions, designed to provide them with opportunities to develop their social and communication skills. Supported by staff and volunteers, they are able to play and socialise in a safe and supportive environment, with other children with additional needs and their siblings. As one mum of four commented, 'I have built up a good support network of friends in a similar situation as myself and family. I have also learned new skills whilst my children are happy and safe.'

Looking to the future

We have identified that an important development for the future will be to further help parents/carers to support their children's learning. One of the areas we are currently developing is the use of the PECS (Picture Exchange Communication System) materials that help children who have limited oral language to communicate more easily. A number of parents and staff have attended training in the use of these materials, which are used to support 'Juskidz' sessions, thereby linking the group with the children's experience at their schools.

We are also planning to extend the course to include skills needed to manage a community group. As well as providing opportunities for individual development for learners, this will support the work of the 'Juskidz' group as a whole and help them to develop their role in the community.

Progression of learners so far has taken place within 'Juskidz'. All eight parents/carers who attended last year's programme have re-enrolled for this year, plus two additional parents/carers. The learners have progressed from a stage when the programme was established where they felt ready to re-engage with learning, to one where they have developed enough confidence to address their own personal and social development and to work towards gaining formal accreditation.

It is our ongoing challenge to ensure that 'Juskidz' is delivered in a way that is informal and flexible enough to meet the complex needs of the learners, while making sure it is a quality learning programme. We use Knowsley FACE's quality improvement procedures, which include following identified procedures for learner induction, registration and support, the use of individual learning plans, the identification and provision of support for learners' individual needs, the use of a comprehensive scheme of work and adherence to Knowsley FACE's guidelines on equal opportunities and diversity.

How and what we've learned

We monitor the programme through the provision of learner information and data collected on the Knowsley FACE Management Information System (MIS), the provision of formal feedback from learners, and through observation of teaching and learning. We supplement these formal procedures with regular informal meetings with the course tutor and learners from the programme, providing good opportunities for learner consultation. There is a formal annual course review of 'Juskidz' at the end of each academic year, which feeds into the Knowsley FACE annual self-assessment process.

One crucial factor to our success has been the willingness on the part of our team to allow the partnership to develop over time, rather than trying to move at an unrealistic pace. Also key are the regular review meetings where Juskidz representatives, the course tutor and the family learning team review the current progress of the programme and plan for its future development. The ability of the tutor and classroom assistant to work flexibly and responsively, to cope with the unexpected and to build excellent relationships with learners, has also been fundamental to the success of the programme.

Cameo 12: St Helens Adult and Community Learning Service

All learning should be enjoyable and the 'Learning through play' course, offered by St Helens Adult and Community Learning Service, provides a strong foundation of learning in a fun and innovative way. The course includes sessions on sensory play, treasure baskets, messy play, communication, relationships, physical development and using the environment. It helps parents and carers to appreciate the importance of their role in providing play opportunities for their children, and the vital part they play in helping their child to have confidence, self-esteem and a real urge to discover. Children's Centres make ideal venues for this course, being spacious and accessible with a friendly atmosphere.

Marlaine Whitham and Sue Morris, St Helens Adult and Community Learning Service

Cameo 13: Bournemouth Adult Learning

Even though it has been running for over 5 years now, Pokesdown Community School's 'Fun with Words' course could have been written with the *Every Child Matters* outcome of 'enjoy and achieve' in mind. It is aimed at Reception children and their parents, who want to explore working together on literacy skills in a fun and relaxed setting at school. The weekly programmes are generally thematic and each parent hour links neatly into the child/parent session that follows. Sessions have included a mini theatre project where children choose a favourite story, parents write a script; they build a 'shoebox theatre' together (complete with moving characters and scenery) and then perform the play.

Jillian Jeffreys, Bournemouth Adult Learning

Cameo 14: Worcestershire County Council Family Learning

Worcestershire County Council's superb outdoor centre at the foot of the Malvern Hills is the setting for a family learning weekend. The aim of the weekend is to give the families a learning experience outdoors, and to show them that they can have fun together, cheaply, or even for free. The families are encouraged to come with all members, including dads and siblings. Together, they take part in many of the outdoor activities available at the centre, including high and low ropes, tunnels, orienteering and photo trails. There are also some indoor workshops in the form of a storyteller followed by an art workshop, a drum workshop, digital cameras and the use of laptops. At the end of the weekend, all achievement – adults' and children's – is recognised by a certificate presented formally by the Centre Instructor.

Jill Allbut, Worcestershire County Council Family Learning

Make a positive contribution

The *Every Child Matters* framework defines 'Making a positive contribution' in the following ways:

- Engaging in decision-making and supporting the community and environment
- Engaging in law-abiding and positive behaviour in and out of school
- Developing positive relationships and choosing not to bully and discriminate
- Developing self-confidence and successfully dealing with significant life changes and challenges
- Developing enterprising behaviour
- Parents, carers and families promoting positive behaviour

Introduction to 'Make a positive contribution'

Anne-Marie Spencer and Clare Meade

Local Authorities are charged with producing Children and Young People's plans that link with the *Every Child Matters* and Youth Matters agendas. However a recent analysis of these plans, by the National Foundation for Educational Research (NFER) (Lord *et al.*, 2006) identified that the education and/or training for parents, carers and families was one of the least referenced actions. Effective partnerships with family learning providers can help to address this omission, as the primary aim of family learning programmes is to engage families in learning together.

With the often negative images in the media of antisocial behaviour, drug and alcohol abuse it is easy to get a one-sided view of children and young people. We can quickly identify antisocial behaviour but it is often harder to identify and encourage positive social behaviour. We need to be clear about the steps we can make which help support children and young people to contribute positively to society. The question is how can we encourage positive social behaviour?

The *Every Child Matters* framework offers us clear ways of identifying, nurturing and encouraging social behaviour. Family learning practitioners can play an important role in contributing to this process.

Through family learning, we help to support the development of parent/child and school relationships. We aim to help parents improve their skills in areas such as literacy, language and numeracy, as well as enhancing their confidence and self-esteem so that they are more able to support their children's learning and to access information and advice when needed.

All of these can help to nurture a more positive environment for the child. The example here, of Wakefield's Family Social and Emotional Aspects of Learning (SEAL) project shows how parents and carers can help to develop children's social, emotional and behavioural skills.

Where children and parents feel positive about their social, emotional and behavioural skills, and are within an environment supportive to emotional health and well-being, they will be better equipped to make and sustain friendships and relationships, and to deal with conflict effectively and fairly. They will be motivated to work and participate in leisure co-operatively, and to compete fairly – winning and losing with dignity and respect for competitors. They are more likely to recognise and stand up for their rights and the rights of others, and to understand and value the differences and commonalities between people.

Through family learning, children and their parents are enabled to make a positive contribution; this could be by working on a specific project that contributes to the local environment, exploring how to support children with decision making, or by demonstrating the effects on behaviour of positive praise and appropriate rewards.

Making a positive contribution: Family SEAL

Anne-Marie Spencer, Skills for Families Consultant, Wakefield Skills for Families

I used the footprints when my children were falling out over sharing their pens and paper. I asked them both to stand facing each other and stand on the footprints. I told them I had learned something in Family SEAL that I would like to try. I asked my son how it would feel if my daughter wouldn't let him join in with the painting she had been doing. He said, 'I would feel sad and upset'. I then asked my daughter how she would feel if her brother wouldn't share his things with her – 'sad' she said.

(A family learning parent)

Family SEAL

At Wakefield Skills for Families (SfF), we have 'piggy-backed' onto the Social and Emotional Aspects of Learning (SEAL) curriculum increasingly being used in primary schools. This is a whole school approach to improving children's social, emotional and behavioural skills. We developed Family SEAL to support parents to learn and use the same approaches taught in school to promote social and emotional well-being and positive behaviour so that there is consistency and increased understanding between home and school. The course is mapped to the adult literacy core curriculum, and parents have an opportunity to gain an Open College accreditation called 'Parenting Matters'.

Seven themes are covered by the SEAL course:

- New beginnings: empathy, self-awareness, motivation, social skills
- Getting on and falling out: managing feelings, empathy, social skills
- Say no to bullying: empathy, self-awareness, social skills
- Going for goals: motivation, self-awareness
- Good to be me: self-awareness, managing feelings, empathy
- Relationships: self-awareness, managing feelings, empathy
- Changes: motivation, social skills, managing feelings

The development of Family SEAL started with training from the Primary Consultant leading the initiative in schools. However, from this, development was slow because of the amount of material available. Whereas schools follow a theme over an academic year and build on this as the children move up through school, Family SEAL is delivered over a twelve-week period to parents who potentially have children in a range of year groups. We had to give considerable thought to how we used the resources most effectively, there was a risk that the themes might not link as well as they should, particularly in the first run of the course.

We chose to deliver the themes through various strands, such as 'What are the social and emotional aspects of learning and why should we focus on them?', 'What are social and emotional behavioural skills?' and 'What vocabulary is focused on in school and what are the key ideas and how are they used?'. These strands give parents a 'flavour' of the themes so that they have a good understanding of what and how the themes are taught to the children and how they could best support the same strategies at home.

Improvements made during the second run of the course included parents attending a SEAL assembly at the start and end of a theme. This has enabled them to link the learning. Some schools have been able to support the course with a learning mentor to reinforce key messages.

Parents joining the course learn how to support their children's developing skills by sharing ideas that recognise and respect their family values and beliefs. They agree 'ground rules' based on this at the start of the course. This approach has been particularly valuable when working in schools with a high proportion of second language children and parents. Through discussion, we explore cultural differences in managing children's behaviour and displays of emotion. These are recognised and valued, and we make sure that the strategies for parents to use in the home are appropriate to individual families and practised through role play and activities in the session before parents use them at home with their children. When parents have had chance to use the strategies, they feed back their successes and challenges at the beginning of the next session.

Parents gain a lot from being able to share experiences. In particular, 'loss' evokes strong emotions from some of the parents, and this has to be managed sensitively. Bullying for some parents is again an emotive theme, parents express their own feelings about being bullied or, for some, being the bullies. It has become apparent that many parents who have been bullied themselves will tell their children to 'stand up for themselves' and hit other children. Through Family SEAL, parents are able to reflect on this cycle of behaviour.

Parents progress to a variety of learning opportunities at the local Adult and Community Education centres or the college. However, many parents are not always ready to take this step and request other family learning courses, such as 'Maths is Magic' or 'Playing with Language', which enable them to learn 'what and how' their children are taught in the literacy or numeracy hour. All family learning courses include a 'Next Steps' progression session, delivered by the family learning teacher, exploring parents' interests, aspirations, family commitments and potential for progressing onto family literacy, language or numeracy programmes or other learning and training programmes. The session also includes how to navigate a prospectus.

Working with schools

As Wakefield's Skills for Families Consultant, I manage the family learning curriculum and sit on the SEAL Strategy Group, attended by a range of services working as part of a multi-disciplinary team. Meetings take place termly to discuss, share and plan a coordinated approach to working with children and parents on the SEAL initiative.

Once a school has applied for a family learning programme a senior member of the family learning team will visit the school to provide an overview of the course, discuss crèche provision and funding available and will undertake a health and safety check and complete a family learning contract. A family learning teacher is then allocated to work with the school. At the initial planning meeting the teacher will ensure the Family SEAL (or other FL) course is in line with the school's development plan. The school will either target a cohort of parents from a particular year group or, where recruitment is particularly challenging, they will target either a key stage or even the whole school!

Cameo 15: West Sussex County Council

West Sussex County Council encourages parents to help in their children's schools, thereby setting a positive example to the children and being more involved in their learning. The Adult Learning Service supports this by offering an OCN-accredited course for parents who help in school. The 20-hour course includes topics such as confidentiality, the organisation of a school and teaching methods. The programme also helps to identify parents with literacy and numeracy needs, and to encourage them to attend basic skills provision, sometimes within the school setting.

Jo Downes, West Sussex County Council

Cameo 16: Hampshire County Council

Hampshire County Council's Adult and Community Learning Service runs the programme, 'Learning together about children's rights', for parents and carers of children aged five to eleven years. The programme raises awareness amongst families about the United Nations Convention on the Rights of the Child. Parents are encouraged to support their child to learn more about rights and responsibilities; and parents' skills are extended to enable them to support their child's speaking, listening and social skills. Often lively and interactive debates encourage the parents and carers to explore the implications of children's rights both for their children and for themselves.

Julia Gahagan, Hampshire County Council Adult and Community Learning Service

Achieve economic well-being

The *Every Child Matters* framework defines 'achieving economic well-being' in the following ways:

- Engaging in further education, employment or training on leaving school
- Being ready for employment
- Living in decent homes and sustainable communities
- Having access to transport and material goods
- Living in households free from low income
- Parents, carers and families are supported to be economically active

Introduction to 'Achieve economic well-being'

Yvonne Casswell, Family Learning Strategy Officer, Leicestershire Adult Learning Service

It is well known that children raised in poverty are more likely to underachieve educationally and that they often grow up to become economically underachieving adults, because they are less prepared for the world of work. We sometimes tend to think of economic well-being as being about family income alone. However, it is inextricably linked to the other interrelated *Every Child Matters* themes. Socio-economic disadvantages in families and communities create major obstacles to all facets of well-being.

Family learning has the potential to be a catalyst for change in promoting economic well-being in a number of ways. It seeks to reduce social exclusion by providing free opportunities for economically disadvantaged families to learn in their local communities; it utilises the motivation of parents to do their best for their children, and provides a non-threatening first step back into learning. Parents gain confidence, motivation and skills and develop their time management skills.

Through family learning, parents and carers identify the skills they need to develop and are motivated to improve their skills and to gain accreditation, often their first successful educational experience.

As parents' confidence increases, so do expectations for themselves and their understanding of how best to support their children's learning. They have access to information, advice and guidance on other learning opportunities, training or employment, and this helps develop clearer employment and personal goals, with a better understanding of how they can achieve these. Family learning is very effective in giving parents/carers the skills and confidence to apply for and sustain training and jobs in different sectors.

Family learning has an impact on whole families: good practice is replicated with other siblings; parents become positive role models, showing how learning can be fun and rewarding, and creating more positive attitudes to learning.

The following examples show how family learning can be powerful in starting parents and carers on their learning journeys, often leading to employment – an aspiration which also maps on to government strategies such as the

Department for Work and Pensions' Five Year Strategy for welfare reform, the *Refugee Employment Strategy* (DWP, 2005b) and the *2005 Skills Strategy* (HM Government, 2005a). In the short term they may find work, move to a better job, gain voluntary work experience or take up further learning. In the medium term, family learning raises aspirations for parents/carers and their children. In the long term, it helps to break the cycle of disadvantage.

Economic well-being: changing prospects

Yvonne Casswell, Family Learning Strategy Officer, Leicestershire Adult Learning Service

Connecting with schools

In Leicestershire, we target our Family Literacy, Language and Numeracy (FLLN) work in communities with high levels of deprivation, recruiting adults with few or no qualifications. Our tutors work with schools where the parents' skills needs are apparent and all the school staff recognise the benefits of family learning and are committed to ensuring its delivery. Here, we explore the work we are doing with one such school – Westfield Infants School in Hinckley.

At Westfield Infants School, we deliver FLLN in 'Keeping Up With The Children'-style courses. The initial 6-week (12-hour) courses are often extended for learners to explore the curriculum in greater depth and to prepare for national tests in literacy and numeracy. The programmes are advertised through fliers and letters from the head teacher, but the understanding and support from all the school's staff are instrumental in positively encouraging those parents, who would most benefit, to attend.

A Saturday open day during National Family Learning Week in October has proved to be an effective way of recruiting parents. The morning starts with a breakfast and ends with an entertainer. We provide literacy and numeracy workshops for parents along with other activities and displays.

Programmes are held in the community centre adjacent to the school for daytime classes, and in the school itself for evening programmes. We give parents resources to use with their children at home, as well as homework to encourage them to work independently to improve their skills, or to try out with their children.

Marion, the Family Learning Tutor, is an accepted and valued member of the school team, visiting frequently to ensure she is familiar with curriculum and school issues, and attending open evenings and parents' evenings to promote the work jointly with school teachers. Jill MacLauchlan, the headteacher of Westfield Infants School, encourages a whole school approach to parental involvement, and Marion works closely with the school staff to develop and provide the programmes.

The initial self-assessment tool, linked to parents' understanding of the National Literacy and Numeracy Strategies identifies learners' starting points while diagnostic assessment identifies more specific targets. A 'Potted History' activity gives information about their past experience of education.

During the weekly sessions, Marion links the topics to the children's curriculum, starting with Reception and working through Key Stage1 to Key Stage 2. She encourages interaction and discussion and the programmes are learner-led. Sessions are fun, with time to explore difficulties, 'no one is rushed', and individual tutorials are offered at the end of the sessions.

The programmes give parents the opportunity to develop their literacy, language and numeracy skills, to get up-to-date with new methods and vocabulary, and to understand how to support their child. They give a real chance to gain confidence in a school environment, share ideas with others, discuss issues with teachers and to think about how to apply their learning in other settings.

The programmes end with a celebration assembly, where parents receive attendance certificates and goody bags. All parents in the school are invited to attend these assemblies, helping with recruitment for future courses.

Our family learning tutors link with Nextstep advisers, inviting them to their groups, and are able to provide information on other programmes and other providers. Some learners move on to further Skills for Life provision to gain Level 2, some move on to FE colleges and take courses such as NVQ2/3 'Childcare and Learning Development' and 'Classroom Assistant' courses.

Other learners, such as Sally, have progressed from family learning to find a new career.

As a single parent with two primary school boys, Sally re-started her learning journey through attending 'Keeping Up With The Children' numeracy and literacy programmes. Her initial motivation for attending was to help and support her children's learning.

She sat and passed Adult Literacy Level 2 and also discovered a talent for Art. She and the rest of the group were privileged to have their paintings exhibited in the local library.

Through further family learning, Sally gained key skills accreditation and a place at De Montfort University on a one year's Access course to study Mathematics and ICT. Although she was unable to draw on financial assistance, she was undaunted, and received her graduation certificate at the end of the year. She was offered the opportunity to study for an HND qualification, but decided against it, as she wanted to begin a career and to be 'off benefits'.

Following further family learning and guidance from our Nextstep advisers, Sally decided to become a plumber. She was accepted on the course – the only female in a group of fifteen men. She gained her qualification, and succeeded in finding a placement as a trainee with an experienced local plumber (which many people struggle to find.)

Through family learning, Sally achieved her goal – 'to get off benefits and have a full-time career':

'Going back to learning has completely changed my life for the better, not only because I am working, but that I have something to offer now. I also feel that I know a lot more about me as a person than I did before. I feel complete'

As well as moving on to further learning and to employment, learners also become more involved with school activities, thereby helping to generate positive attitudes to learning in their children. Westfield Infants School runs a successful 'Right to Read' (R2R) programme, and 15 of the current 19 volunteers on the programme are ex-family learning learners. The R2R consultant is impressed with the number of parent/carer volunteers at the school and has asked to share this good practice with other schools.

The school staff recognise the value of family learning to both parents/carers and their children. They report parents' increased confidence in supporting their children with maths homework and using current calculation strategies, as well as increased use of games that support phonics and literacy for all children, but particularly for those on the SEN record. Comments in home/school reading contact books show more specific understanding of the reading process and teachers also report improved relationships between children and R2R volunteers.

Managing the provision

In 2003, we appointed five Family Learning Development Tutors to develop FLLN. These tutors are based in the county working in areas of high deprivation. Tutors build links with local schools and negotiate programmes to suit learners' and schools' needs. We work with the Primary Strategy team of Leicestershire County Council who can advise on curriculum issues, and we have a team of community development workers who work in targeted wards to identify community needs. This information, along with the statistical data, informs the location and style of delivery.

The Family Learning Strategy Officer manages the FLLN provision. The Family Learning Development Tutors form the core of the delivery team, together with Skills for Life and ESOL sessional tutors. The team meets on a monthly basis to share good practice, develop the curriculum and discuss on-going issues. The tutors who are based in various locations across the county maintain additional regular contact through email, shared training, visits and meetings.

The Family Learning Strategy Officer works closely with the Skills for Life Strategy Officer, as there are many common training, resource and progression issues. We also work with other officers and senior managers within Leicestershire Adult Learning Service to develop a coherent strategy for adult learning development and provision in the county. Family learning links to the other significant strands of adult learning delivery, namely employability and widening participation in communities of high deprivation. We constantly review and prioritise areas for development, for example our recruitment strategy with the aim of involving more men in FLLN.

The greatest challenge for our service has been to raise the profile of FLLN within Children's Services and to demonstrate the benefits of FLLN in raising children's achievement and fostering positive attitudes to learning. Tutors spend time building and maintaining relationships with schools, but other issues, such as change of school staff, Ofsted inspection or refurbishment can lead to postponement. Additional work is needed to engage new parents where the programmes are not firmly established. We have found that the most important ingredient in success or otherwise of a programme is the understanding and commitment of the head teacher, and through him/her, other key school staff.

Cameo 17: Lancashire Adult Learning

The Adult College, Lancaster has developed a family learning programme in some of Fleetwood's areas of high deprivation. The programme was developed as a pilot in two primary schools. Initial contact with parents was through either a 12-hour 'Keeping Up With the Children' course or a 12-hour programme looking at the role of parents in school. The majority of the learners, both parents and grandparents, had left school with no qualifications and had negative experiences of their own schooling. Family learning provided the first opportunity for them to return to learning, and many progressed to further FLLN or Skills for Life programmes (some of which were specially set up in a local community centre) and to achieve Level 1 and Level 2 adult literacy and numeracy certificates.

The college also runs workplace NVQ programmes for teaching assistants and this has enabled parents from FLLN programmes, who are interested in working in schools, to progress on to either a VQ or NVQ for teaching assistants. This has been particularly enhanced by the introduction of 12-hour 'Step into Childcare' VQ as a bridging programme between FLLN and the NVQ.

Mandy Williams, Lancashire Adult Learning

Cameo 18: Redbridge Institute of Adult Education

Somali families in Redbridge were identified by the local Refugee Forum as having a particular interest in developing sewing skills for personal projects, and as needing skills to enhance adults' employability. Redbridge Institute of Adult Education's Wider Family Learning Service, together with the Refugee Forum, developed 'Sewing for Somali Families'. The course venue and timing were negotiated to fit in with families as much as possible. The course was held near the main Ilford shopping centre on alternate Saturday mornings.

Families learned how to adapt commercial patterns and cut material and many used a sewing machine for the first time. The course also helped adults and children to improve their numeracy skills by taking measurements and measuring and estimating fabrics. Budgeting skills were incorporated by families doing their own shopping for material. Language barriers were overcome by using a volunteer from the Somali Consortium as an interpreter. Adults also improved their English spoken skills and learned new vocabulary.

Maria Sotiriou, Redbridge Institute of Adult Education

Cameo 19: Kingston Adult Education

Kingston Adult Education Family Learning delivered a 'Springboard' course at a local Children's Centre in July 2006. The 5-session course was designed to attract parent/carers who had been on previous family learning courses at the children's centre as a progression route. It was delivered by two teachers and a local Connexions advisor. Parents were offered one to one advice and guidance sessions where they discussed further learning and employment opportunities. They were shown how to complete CVs and were given support with IT skills. An outreach officer from the Children's Information Service came to talk to the group about working in childcare and child tax credits. As a result of this course some parents moved on to further learning, including GCSE English and horticulture, while others moved into employment in childcare.

Veronica Storey, Kingston Adult Education

Section 5
QUALITY MATTERS

Quality Matters: an introduction

Penny Lamb

As the minister says in the foreword to this book, when we are working with some of the most vunerable families in the country, it is critical that we know that they will receive a high quality learning experience the first time they walk through the door. We have to be sure that each and every learning session is exciting, fun and that learning takes place in a way that meets the individual needs of the learners and achieves the objectives of the programme. The starting point of new learning journeys must also ensure that learners want to return and progress on to other learning opportunities. In many cases, the focus of attracting parents and carers back into learning to support their children is a powerful incentive, so powerful that it often overcomes extreme fears, school-phobia and previous negative learning experiences. Local quality improvement systems need to ensure that at the point of entry and throughout the programmes learners are guaranteed an effective learning experience. This should be backed by regulatory checks by external agencies, through inspection and monitoring from funding agencies. This chapter provides a brief overview.

Local quality improvement systems

Local quality improvement systems focus on a number of key areas of a learner's journey and of the leadership and management of programmes. These include recruitment; induction; observation of teaching and learning; staff training and continuous professional development; the review and evaluation of programmes; the gathering of learner and partner feedback; the analysis of data and participation rates in relation to strategic aims; gathering systematic data on progression; ensuring effective promotion of quality and diversity; ensuring value for money; effective systems for initial assessment; review; self assessment; and sharing of good practice. These local systems fit into much wider quality and regulatory frameworks that focus around the adult as a learner, the outcomes of the *Every Child Matters* agenda and the monitoring and assessment of local authority provision.

Inspection

All family learning programmes funded through the Learning and Skills Council are subject to inspection from the Office of Standards in Education, Children's Services and Skills, more commonly known as the new Ofsted. The new Ofsted was formed in April 2007 and has taken on the responsibilities of the Adult Learning Inspectorate; the work of the Commission for Social Care Inspection (CSCI) that relates to children; the work of HM Inspectorate of Court Administration (HMICA) that relates to the children and family courts; as well as the work of the previous Ofsted.

The inspection of post-16 learning, excluding higher education, is subject to a quality framework, known as the Common Inspection Framework. It asks one fundamental question on the overall effectiveness of the provision:

> *How effective and efficient are the provision and related services in meeting the full range of learners' needs and why?*

The framework places the experience of the learner at the core. It has five key areas of inspection:

- How well do learners achieve?
- How effective are teaching, training and learning?
- How well do programmes and activities meet the needs and interests of learners?
- How well are learners guided and supported?
- How effective are leadership and management in raising achievement and supporting all learners?

Each key question is cross-referenced to the *Every Child Matters* outcomes for young people and vulnerable adults. This is an additional critical element for family learning provision.

Current inspections of local authority adult and family learning provision are carried out on a proportionate basis, that is, the level and intensity of the inspection is proportionate to the level of risk to the learners. An outstanding provider will receive a light-touch inspection. Provision inspected under the Common Inspection Framework is graded on the following scale:

- Grade 1 Outstanding
- Grade 2 Good
- Grade 3 Satisfactory
- Grade 4 Inadequate

In 2005–06, 55 per cent of family learning provision inspected by the Adult Learning Inspectorate was judged to be good or better, with the rest satisfactory. (ALI, 2006). These are consistently higher grades than other areas of the adult learning sector.

Whilst the current new Ofsted inspection regime for LSC-funded family programmes concentrates on the learning outcomes for the adults, there is an expectation that providers will also capture and measure the children's achievement, as this a key underpinning principle of the programmes. Family learning is not treated as a curriculum area, but as a separate way of providing courses that crosses a number of curriculum areas. It is currently inspected and reported on as a unique area in its own right. In addition to the requirements of the inspectorate, quality issues are also addressed in the LSC's annual guidance to support the process and timetabling for planning funding and delivery of family programmes.

Family learning provision contributes to a number of other key strategic areas, and as such often features in other inspections as well. A recent review of the number of regulatory and advisory frameworks used across family learning and parenting skills programmes in multi-agency settings revealed 27 different frameworks. For family learning programmes in local authority settings, the additional key regulatory frameworks are currently Joint Area Reviews (JARs), Annual Performance Assessments (APA) and Comprehensive Performance Assessment (CPA).

JARs, APAs and CPAs

Joint Area Reviews and Annual Performance Assessments are two complementary elements of the overall children's services inspection process. The *Framework for the inspection of children's services* defines principles to be applied in all relevant inspections of services for children and young people, which include JARs, APAs and other inspections, such as those of schools and children's homes. It sets out how inspections will report on the contributions of services to improving the five outcomes for children and young people in terms of their: being healthy; staying safe; enjoying and achieving; making a positive contribution; and achieving economic well-being and includes the support given to parents and carers.

Family learning services across England have been involved in the joint area review processes in different ways. In some cases, this has included case studies on specific themes, for others this has been discussion on the children's achievement from the programmes or visits to groups of parents and carers to assess their involvement. Through the JAR process, each of the Every Child Matters outcomes is graded, using the reverse scale to the Common Inspection Framework:

- Grade 4 Outstanding
- Grade 3 Good
- Grade 2 Adequate
- Grade 1 Inadequate

The Audit Commission assesses the performance of local authorities and the services that they provide for local people to help focus on improvement currently through the Comprehensive Performance Assessment (CPA). The essence of the CPA framework is that it draws on a range of information such as performance indicators, assessments of corporate capacity, audit and inspection reports, and stakeholder opinions, to reach a single judgement about the performance of a local body. CPA, JARs and APAs will not continue beyond March 2009. These will be replaced by a system of Comprehensive Area Assessment (CAA). CAA will focus on outcomes for places rather than just the individual bodies responsible for local services. It will look across local government, housing, health, education and community safety. The new CAA framework will cover all local public services. It aims to provide a more joined-up and proportionate approach to public service regulation.

As the profile of family learning and working with parents increases within the policy agenda, the need to ensure that effective quality improvement systems are in place for all provision, irrespective of funding stream will become increasingly critical. The case studies on earlier pages provide an effective demonstration of quality provision. The following case study illustrates how Cheshire County Council has ensured a strategic approach to quality improvement through the local use of a quality kite mark.

Further information on inspection and quality can be found at:

http://www.audit-commission.gov.uk

http://www.campaign-for-learning.org.uk/familylearningnetwork

http://dcsf.gov.uk/readwriteplus

http://www.lluk.org

http://www.lsc.gov.uk

http://www.niace.org.uk/Research/Family

http://www.ofsted.gov.uk

http://www.qia.org.uk

Developing a quality framework for family learning: the Cheshire model

Pauline Kershaw, Family Learning Manager

Phase 1: 2004–2007 Cheshire Quality Standards Kite Mark for Family Learning

Developing the quality standards for family learning in Cheshire provided us with two key outcomes: a county-wide understanding across a range of providers of the policy, strategy and standards for family learning; and a quality process to put policy into practice to the benefit of ALL families who attend family learning provision spanning all providers and locations.

We identified the following key success factors in establishing and embedding the quality standards:

- the partnership approach to family learning across providers strategically led by the Family Learning Reference Group;
- the development of policy, strategy and standards to underpin the kite marking process;
- a pilot phase of testing the evidence base against the standards with a range of providers;
- a professionally produced guidance folder signed by the Director for Education and Community;
- a high-profile launch;
- a dedicated family learning team with appropriate skills to support partners in developing the portfolio of evidence.

Why did Cheshire introduce a Quality Kite Mark?

Cheshire is very fortunate to have such a wide range of partners who are working hard to develop family learning provision. There are five FE colleges, over a hundred schools, five local SureStarts and a number of voluntary and community sector providers involved in the partnership. This is good news for learners because it means that there is so much more choice on offer. The key objective is to ensure continuous improvement in all aspects of family learning provision, wherever and by whichever provider it is delivered.

How did Cheshire develop the Quality Kite Mark?

During 2004 the County Family Learning Reference Group agreed that maintaining quality was a priority; as a result a small group of colleagues, representing a range of providers from local SureStarts, FE colleges, community and voluntary sector, schools and parenting support providers, worked together to develop the Quality Kite Mark. The intention was that a Kite Mark would assist in monitoring provision against the four key aims outlined in the Cheshire policy, strategy and standards, which had previously been developed and agreed by partners. The standards meet the five key questions outlined in the Common Inspection Framework.

The group, led by the Family Learning Manager, decided that an evidenced based portfolio building approach would lend itself to supporting the process. The working group analysed the quality standards and thought carefully about how this could be evidenced across the range of types of providers.

It was decided that each key provider would need its own set of guidance notes.

The Quality Kite Mark portfolio guidance folders were put together with this in mind. The group also worked out a step-by-step approach to the process. Each representative from the key providers offered to trial the portfolio building process. This reassured the group that building an evidence base against the quality standards could be achieved with relative ease within their own context. Thus they had the knowledge that the kite marking process worked effectively for a range of providers. This pragmatic approach proved to be a winner and was later used as an important lever in persuading other providers to follow suit.

Phase 2: 2005/6 A regional approach

The North West Family Learning Forum Quality Standards Kite Mark and 'The Building Blocks of Quality in Family Learning'

The North West Family Learning Forum has been in existence for over 15 years, with a specific remit for sharing good practice across Local Authority family learning provision. Members were interested in finding ways of implementing the framework approach in the *The Building Blocks of quality in Family Learning*, (Haggart and Spacey, 2006b) They also wanted to further develop Cheshire's Kite Marked approach, in order to support the quality improvement agenda across the North West region. The Cheshire Family Learning Manager led a writing group, which included representatives from the local authorities of Warrington, Lancashire, St Helens, Wirral and Cheshire, the NIACE Family Learning Development Officer and a Campaign for Learning representative. The group worked collectively during 2006 on producing the final published document *The North West Family Learning Forum Quality Standards Kitemark.* The work of the group involved:

- reviewing the Cheshire standards and mapping to the five key aims outlined in *The Building Blocks of Quality in Family Learning*;
- reaching agreement on the process of kite marking and regional moderation support process;
- reaching agreement on the format and wording of the guidance document for providers;
- commissioning Cheshire to publish the final document and CD;
- gaining support of the full membership of the Regional North West Family Learning forum;
- gaining national endorsement from NIACE and Campaign for Learning.

The North West Family Learning Forum Quality Standards Kite Mark was launched in December 2006.

Next steps: Supporting quality in parenting skills

There is significant interest nationally in improving the quality of group-based parenting skills programmes in line with the Common Inspection Framework. The DIUS has commissioned NIACE to review *The Building Blocks of quality in Family Learning* and to produce a new quality guide that covers family learning and group parenting skills programmes. In Cheshire, we will build this into our quality framework systems.

FURTHER INFORMATION

Partnership

One of the key strengths of family learning programmes is the range of organisations they work with. In connecting family learning with the *Every Child Matters* agenda, it can be useful to explore the possibility of partnership with organisations such as:

- Board of Prison Visitors
- Children's Centres
- Children's Information Services
- Connexions
- Drugs workers and voluntary organisations
- Fire safety officers
- Job Centre Plus
- Local arts bodies, such as theatres, museums, art galleries
- Local authority children's services departments
- Local community and voluntary groups, such as Refugee Forum
- Local community centres
- Local health and fitness clubs (eg football club)
- Local Healthy Schools
- Local Primary Care Trust
- Local regeneration projects
- Local schools
- Other curriculum areas within your provision
- Outdoors centres
- Police service
- Road safety teams
- Safer School Partnerships
- School Inclusion teams
- SureStart
- Victim Support Service
- Youth offending teams

Funding

Sources of funding for family learning projects connecting with the *Every Child Matters* agenda, might include:

* Awards for All
* The Big Lottery Fund
* Department of Health Section 64 funding (voluntary sector)
* European Social Fund
* Job Centre Plus
* Local antisocial behaviour partnerships
* Local Primary Care Trust (PCT)
* Local regeneration projects
* Local SureStart
* LSC FLLN/FL
* Neighbourhood Learning for Deprived Communities
* Paul Hamlyn Foundation
* Sport England
* Youth Offending Service

Useful websites

www.antibullying.net
Information for young people, parents and teachers on tackling bullying within schools.

http://www.audit-commission.gov.uk
Website of the Audit Commission, the independent public body that assesses the performance of local authorities and other local public services. For information on CPA/CAA and APA.

www.awardsforall.org.uk
Awards for All Lottery grants scheme.

www.biglotteryfund.org.uk
Information about funding currently available from the Big Lottery Fund.

www.campaign-for-learning.org.uk
Website of the Campaign for Learning.

www.campaign-for-learning.org.uk/familylearningnetwork
Website of the Family Learning Network, a network of family learning
practitioners. For general information and updates on family learning.

www.communities.gov.uk
Website of the Department of Communities and Local Government.

www.dcsf.gov.uk/readwriteplus
Website of the Basic Skills Strategy Unit. For information on quality in Family
Literacy, Language and Numeracy programmes.

www.dcsf.gov.uk/skillsstrategy
Government Skills Strategy website, providing information on the national skills
agenda.

www.dwp.gov.uk/welfarereform
Department for Work and Pensions' website on the welfare reform agenda.

www.employabilityforum.co.uk
Website of the Employability Forum, an independent organisation that promotes
the employment of refugees and the integration of migrant workers in the UK.

www.everychildmatters.gov.uk
A web portal for resources and information relating to *Every Child Matters*.

www.healthystart.nhs.uk
Information about the Healthy Start scheme.

www.hlf.org.uk
Heritage Lottery Fund.

www.iagreview.org.uk
Website of the partners undertaking the review of Information, Advice and
Guidance, as recommended in the 2005 Skills White Paper.

www.knowyourlimits.gov.uk/stay_safe
Information on alcohol and related issues.

www.healthyschools.gov.uk
A web-based directory of local Healthy Schools Programmes.

www.lluk.org
Website of Lifelong Learning UK, the sector skills agency for the learning and skills sector. For information on the national occupational standards for family learning.

www.lsc.gov.uk
Website of the Learning and Skills Council, the body responsible for planning and funding all publicly-funded post-16 learning that is not university education. For information on family programmes funded through the Learning and Skills Council.

www.nhsdirect.nhs.uk
Common health questions answered.

www.ofsted.gov.uk
Website of the new Ofsted, the body charged with inspecting the performance of pre and post-16 learning provision. For information on inspection.

www.niace.org.uk/connect-five
Website of information and additional materials to augment the Connect-five publication.

www.niace.org.uk/Research/Family
Pages of the NIACE website dedicated to NIACE's family learning work. For information on quality, Family Learning Topic Papers, research and publications on family learning.

www.ncb.org.uk/library/cpis
A national information service on children's play based at the National Children's Bureau Library.

www.nspcc.org.uk/kidszone/staysafe.htm
Child-friendly tips on staying safe while having fun.

www.phf.org.uk
The Paul Hamlyn Foundation, independent grant making body.

www.playengland.org.uk
Website of Play England, a five-year project to promote strategies for free play and to create a lasting support structure for play providers in England.

www.qia.org.uk
Website of the Quality Improvement Agency, the body taking forward the Improvement Strategy for the learning and skills sector. For information on quality and examples of best practice.

www.respect.gov.uk
The website for the Government' s Respect drive - tackling anti-social behaviour and its causes.

www.skillsactive.com
The Sector Skills Council for Active Leisure and Learning.

www.sportengland.org
Information about funding currently available from the lottery distributor, Sport England.

www.storybookdads.co.uk
Storybook Dad – an independent charity working in prisons, with the aim of maintaining family ties and facilitating learning for prisoners and their children through the provision of story CDs.

www.yjb.gov.uk
Youth Justice Board information on preventing re-offending by young people.

REFERENCES

ALI (2006) *Adult Learning Inspectorate, Chief Inspector's Report, 2005–06.* Coventry, ALI.

Bentley, T and O'Leary, D (2006) 'Children's Services: the professional challenge' in Capacity (2006) *The learning we live by: education policies for children, families and communities.* London: Capacity.

Cabinet Office (2006) *Reaching out: an action plan on social inclusion.* London: Cabinet Office.

Cabinet Office, Social Exclusion Team (2007) *Reaching out: think family, Analysis and themes from the families at risk review..* London: Cabinet Office.

Children's Play Council (2006) *Planning for play: guidance on the development and implementation of a local play strategy.* London: Big Lottery Fund.

DCMS (2004) *Getting Serious About Play: a review of children's play.* London: Department for Culture, Media and Sports.

DCMS (2006) *Time for play: encouraging greater play opportunities for children and young people.* London: Department for Culture, Media and Sports.

DCSF (2007) *Extended schools: building on experience.* Nottingham: Department for Children, Schools and Families.

Department for Work and Pensions (2005a) *Five Year Strategy: Opportunity and security throughout life.* London: The Stationery Office.

Department for Work and Pensions (2005b) *Working to rebuild lives: a refugee employment strategy.* Sheffield: Department for Work and Pensions.

Department of Health (2002) *Safeguarding children: a joint chief inspectors' report on arrangements to safeguard children.* London: Department of Health.

Department of Health (2004a) *Choosing Health. Making healthy choices easier.* Cm 6374. London: Department of Health.

Department of Health (2004b) *Every Child Matters. Change for children in health services.* London: Department of Health.

Department of Health (2004c) *National Service Framework for Children. Young People and Maternity Services.* London: Department of Health.

DfEE (1998) *The National Literacy Strategy: A Framework for Teaching.* London, Department for Education and Employment.

DfEE (1999a) *The National Numeracy Strategy.* London, Department for Education and Employment.

DfEE (1999b) *A Fresh Start: improving literacy and numeracy.* London, Department for Education and Employment.

DfEE (2001) *Skills for life: the national strategy for improving adult literacy and numeracy.* Nottingham: Department for Education and Employment.

DfES (2004a) *Every Child Matters: change for children in schools.* Nottingham: Department for Education and Skills.

DfES (2004b) *Every Child Matters: change for children in social care.* Nottingham: Department for Education and Skills.

DfES (2004c) *Every Child Matters: next steps.* Nottingham: Department for Education and Skills.

DfES (2004d) *Five year strategy for children and learners. Putting people at the heart of public services.* Nottingham: Department for Education and Skills.

DfES (2004e) *Healthy living blueprint for schools.* Nottingham: Department for Education and Skills.

DfES (2005a) *Common core of skills and knowledge for the children's workforce.* Nottingham: Department for Education and Skills.

DfES (2005b) *Extended schools: access to opportunities and services for all.* Nottingham: Department for Education and Skills.

DfES (2005c) *Family literacy, language and numeracy: a guide for extended schools.* Nottingham: Department for Education and Skills.

DfES (2005d) *National healthy schools status: a guide for schools.* Nottingham: Department for Education and Skills.

DfES (2005e) *Strengthening family literacy, language and numeracy: good practice guidance for planning and delivering joint sessions.* Nottingham: DfES.

DfES (2006a) *Care Matters Transforming the Lives of Children and Young People in Care.* Cm 6932. Norwich: The Stationery Office.

DfES (2006b) *Children's workforce strategy: building a world-class workforce for children, young people and families.* Nottingham: Department for Education and Skills.

DfES (2006c) *Common Assessment Framework: managers' guide.* Nottingham: Department for Education and Skills.

DfES (2006d) *Learning outside the classroom manifesto.* Nottingham: Department for Education and Skills.

DfES (2006e) *Parenting support: guidance for local authorities in England.* Nottingham: Department for Education and Skills.

DfES (2006f) *Planning and funding extended schools: a guide for schools, local authorities and their partner organizations.* Nottingham: Department for Education and Skills.

DfES (2006g) *Safer school partnerships: mainstreaming guidance.* Nottingham: Department for Education and Skills.

DfES (2007a) *Care Matters: time for change.* Cm 7137. Norwich: The Stationery Office.

DfES (2007b) *Every Parent Matters.* Nottingham: Department for Education and Skills.

DfES (2007c) *Governance guidance for SureStart Children's Centres and Extended Schools.* Nottingham: Department for Education and Skills.

DfES and Cabinet Office (2005) *Making a difference: reducing bureaucracy in children, young people and family services.* Nottingham: Department for Education and Skills.

DfES and DCMS (2003) *Learning through PE and sport: a guide to the physical education, schools sport and club links strategy.* Nottingham: Department for Education and Skills.

DfES and DCMS (2004) *Boost for school sport* http://www.teachernet.gov.uk/_doc/7989/boostleaflet.pdf (accessed 27.06.07).

DfES and DoH (2004) *National Service Framework for children, young people and maternity services: supporting local delivery.* London: Department of Health.

DfES and DoH (2006) *SureStart Children's Centres: practice guidance.* Nottingham: DfES.

DfES and DWP (2006) *Choice for parents, the best start for children, making it happen: an action plan for the ten year strategy – Sure Start Children's Centres, extended schools and childcare.* Nottingham: DfES.

Haggart, J and Spacey, R (2006a) *Linking the thinking in family learning.* Leicester: NIACE.

Haggart, J and Spacey, R (2006b) *The building blocks of quality in family learning: guidance for planners, managers and practitioners.* Leicester, NIACE.

Haggart, J and Spacey, R (2006c) *Adding value: adult learning and extended services.* Leicester, NIACE.

HM Government (1998) *Crime and disorder Act 1998.* Norwich: The Stationery Office.

HM Government (2002) *The Education Act 2002.* Norwich: The Stationery Office.

HM Government (2003) *Every Child Matters.* Cm 5860. Norwich: The Stationery Office.

HM Government (2004a) *Children Act 2004.* Norwich: The Stationery Office.

HM Government (2004b) *Every Child Matters: change for children.* Nottingham: Department for Education and Skills.

HM Government (2005a) *Skills: Getting on in business, getting on at work.* London: The Stationery Office.

HM Government (2005b) *Youth Matters.* Cm 6629. Norwich: The Stationery Office.

Home Office (2004) *Every Child Matters: change for children in the criminal justice system.* Nottingham: Department for Education and Skills.

Home Office (2006) *Respect Action Plan.* London: Home Office.

Interagency Group (2004) *From vision to reality: transforming outcomes for children and families.* London: Local Government Association.

Laming (2003) *The Victoria Climbie Inquiry.* Cm 5730. Norwich: The Stationery Office, .

Lander, V (2006) Guidance for primary student teachers on addressing diversity and EAL issues in the classroom. http://www.multiverse.ac.uk/attachments/ca884b80-9983-4723-b5e7-78e4f5e3d1cd.pdf (accessed 1.02.2007).

Leitch Review of Skills (2006) *Prosperity for all in the global economy: world class skills.* Norwich: The Stationery Office..

Lord, P et al (2006) *Analysis of Children and Young People's Plans 2006.* Slough: NFER.

LSC (2007) *Supplementary guidance and information for Learning and Skills Councils and those managing family programmes.* Coventry: LSC.

NIACE (2007) *Quality Matters: think family, a multi-agency quality guide.* Due for publication Autumn 2007.

Ofsted (2005) *Common Inspection Framework.* London: Ofsted

Ofsted (2005) *Every Child Matters, Framework for the inspection of children's services.* London:Ofsted

Qualifications and Curriculum Authority (2005) *National Standards for Literacy, Numeracy and ICT.* London: QCA.

UN General Assembly (1989) *Convention on the rights of the child* http://www.ohchr.org/english/law/pdf/crc.pdf (accessed 27.06.07)

GLOSSARY

BME   **Black and Minority Ethnic**
CYPP   **Children and Young People's Plan**
The CYPP, which covers the education and social services functions of the local authority, forms the statutory basis for planning Children's Trust arrangements. It includes input from the relevant plans of all partners covered by the duty to co-operate required by the Children Act 2004. This duty to co-operate applies to all agencies dealing with children.

                                              www.everychildmatters.gov.uk

Children's Centre
Places where children under 5 years old and their families can receive seamless holistic integrated services and information, and where they can access help from multi-disciplinary teams of professionals.

                                                    www.surestart.gov.uk

Community cohesion
A cohesive community is defined as one where there is a common vision and a sense of belonging for all communities; the diversity of people's different backgrounds and circumstances is appreciated and positively valued; those from different backgrounds have similar life opportunities; and strong and positive relationships are being developed between people from different backgrounds in the workplace, in schools and within neighbourhoods.

                                              www.communities.gov.uk

Distance learning
Learning at home, with little or no face-to-face contact with teachers and with material provided remotely, e.g. by e-mail, internet, television, or post.

Eid
A Muslim celebratory festival. There are two major Eid in the Muslim calendar: one to celebrate the end of Ramadan, and the other to celebrate the end of the hajj pilgrimage to Mecca.

ESOL   English as a Second or Other Language

www.lsc.gov.uk

ECM   Every Child Matters
An approach to the well-being of children and young people from birth to age 19. Five outcomes for children are placed at the centre of all policies and approaches involving children's services, and it aims to ensure that all providers of services involving children work together in integrated and effective ways.

www.everychildmatters.gov.uk

Family learning
Learning as, or within, a family, where the notion of 'family' encompasses the myriad of forms chosen in contemporary society. Learning that helps people operate as a family.

FLLN   Family Literacy Language and Numeracy
Programmes that use a family learning approach to help adults improve their literacy, language and numeracy skills. Usually funded through the LSC FLLN funding stream.

www.lsc.gov.uk

5-a-day
Government campaign to encourage people to eat more fruit and vegetables.

www.5aday.nhs.uk

Generic learning outcomes
A system of using general groups of learning outcomes to categorise the personal learning outcomes that learners describe and experience.

IAG   Information, Advice and Guidance
Provision of information, advice or guidance to support individuals into learning and work opportunities.

www.lsc.gov.uk/iag

JAR   Joint Area Review
JARs examine how far children and young people in a local authority are achieving the *Every Child Matters* outcomes. They cover all education and social services directly managed or commissioned by a local authority, as well as health and youth justice services provided by partner agencies.

www.ofsted.gov.uk

KUWC Keeping Up With The Children

Keeping up with the children (KUWC) programmes are for parents/carers to become more involved in their children's education by understanding the literacy and numeracy curricula, and improving their own literacy, language or numeracy skills.

www.basic-skills.co.uk

Kids VIP

Kids VIP works to enable relationships between children and their imprisoned parents to be sustained and developed. Kids VIP is the recognised specialist agency concerned with children visiting prison.

LSC Learning and Skills Council

The non-departmental public body responsible for planning and funding high quality education and training for adults in England, other than those in universities.

www.lsc.gov.uk

(Community) Learning champion

Local people recruited to advocate the power of learning to friends and colleagues, and who make contact with other local people who may not have achieved well at school and who are not participating in any other learning programmes.

www.continyou.org.uk

LAA Local Area Agreement

LAAs set out the priorities for a local area agreed between central government and a local area (the local authority and Local Strategic Partnership) and other key partners at the local level.

www.communities.gov.uk

Local play strategies

A 2004 report by the Department for Culture, Media and Sport (DCMS) of a review of children's play in England, recommended that local authorities needed to take the lead in planning for play across their area. Local play strategies should enable local authorities and their partners to invest in play projects that best meet the needs of children in their communities. Consideration of children's need to play should become part of the strategic policy framework for all decisions that affect the planning and design of both children's services and public space into the future.

www.playengland.org.uk

MIS   Management Information System

Matrix Quality Mark
The Matrix Standard is the national quality standard for any organisation that delivers information, advice and/or guidance on learning and work.

www.matrixstandard.com

National Healthy Schools Programme
A partnership between the health service and schools. The programme aims to:
* support children and young people in developing healthy behaviours;
* help to raise pupil achievement;
* help to reduce health inequalities; and
* help promote social inclusion.

Schools are expected to take a 'whole school' approach, involving the whole school community, including parents and carers. They are required to provide evidence that they are meeting the Healthy Schools Standard to promote a coherent and holistic message about the importance of a healthy lifestyle.

www.healthyschools.gov.uk

OCN   Open College Network
The National Open College Network (NOCN) provides national qualifications and programmes in a wide range of subject areas and offers a local accreditation service, through the OCNs, that provides recognition of achievement through the award of credit.

www.nocn.org.uk

PECS   Picture Exchange Communication System
See page 68

www.pecs.org.uk (Pyramid Educational Consultants – home of PECS)

PCT   Primary Care Trust
Funded directly by the Department of Health, Since April 2002, PCTs have taken control of local health care while strategic Health Authorities monitor performance and standards.

www.dh.gov.uk

Ramadan
A Muslim period of daytime fasting and contemplation which lasts for a lunar month of about 28 days.

RARPA Recognising and Recording Progress and Achievement
A learner-focused system of recognising both anticipated and unanticipated learning outcomes arising from non-accredited programmes.

www.lsc.gov.uk/rarpa

R2R   Right to Read
The 'Right to read' project in Leicestershire, one of the largest volunteer projects in the country whereby business people volunteer to go into schools to support pupils who are struggling with their reading.

www.leics-ebc.org.uk (Leicestershire Education Business Company – leads the Leicestershire Right to Read campaign)

Safer School Partnerships
A Safer School Partnership is a collaborative approach between a school, police and other local agencies working towards the following aims:
- to reduce the prevalence of crime, anti-social behaviour and victimisation amongst young people and to reduce the number of incidents and crimes in schools and their wider communities;
- to provide a safe and secure school community which enhances the learning environment;
- to engage young people, challenge unacceptable behaviour, and help them develop a respect for themselves and their community;
- to ensure that young people remain in education, actively learning, healthy and achieving their full potential.

www.everychildmatters.gov.uk

Share
Share uses a practical, 'hands-on' approach to involving parents in their children's learning. Parents and carers work with their children at home using a range of Share materials. Parents/carers can gain OCN accreditation for the work they put into supporting their child's learning.

www.continyou.org.uk

Skills for Families
An initiative that ended in July 2005. Its aim was to develop a coherent, cross-agency approach to area-wide programmes for families, including the development of new programmes to improve the literacy, language and numeracy skills of parents or carers and their children.

www.literacytrust.org.uk

SfL   Skills for Life
The ability to read, write and speak English and to use mathematics at a level necessary to function and progress at work and society in general. This includes ICT and ESOL.

www.dcsf.gov.uk/readwriteplus

SEAL   Social and Emotional Aspects of Learning
See page 75

www.standards.dfes.gov.uk

SEN   Special Educational Needs
The term 'special educational needs' has a legal definition, referring to children who have learning difficulties or disabilities that make it harder for them to learn or access education than most children of the same age.

www.teachernet.gov.uk/wholeschool/sen

SATS   Standard Attainment Tests
Unofficial name for National Curriculum tests for children, set by the Government.

www.qca.org.uk

SureStart
Government programme that aims to deliver the best start in life for every child. It brings together early education, childcare, health and family support.

www.surestart.gov.uk

VQ/NVQ   Vocational Qualification/National Vocational Qualification
Vocational qualifications provide a broad introduction to a particular career or industry sector. National Vocational Qualifications demonstrate the skills and knowledge required for particular occupations.

www.qca.org.uk

Youth Justice Plan
The Crime and Disorder Act 1998 established both the Youth Justice System, which aims to prevent offending by children and young people aged 10 to 17, and a new statutory requirement for local authorities to produce an annual Youth Justice Plan, describing the nature and scale of offending by young people in their area, and the programmes available to tackle it. The Youth Justice Plan is aligned with the Children and Young People's Plan.

www.everychildmatters.gov.uk

Youth Offending Teams

Youth Offending Teams were introduced in 2000. They are comprised of professionals from a range of fields, including local authority social services and education departments, the police, probation service and health authorities. The manager of each Youth Offending Team, coordinates the work of their local youth justice services.

www.everychildmatters.gov.uk